ENGLISH RECUSANT LITERATURE
1558–1640

Selected and Edited by
D. M. ROGERS

Volume 365

ROBERT PERSONS
Newes from Spayne and Holland
1593

RICHARD SMITH
A Brief Inquisition
1630

SAINT BONAVENTURE
The Psalter of the B. Virgin Mary
1624

ROBERT PERSONS

Newes from Spayne and Holland

1593

The Scolar Press
1977

ISBN 0 85967 431 2

Published and printed in Great Britain by
The Scolar Press Limited, 59-61 East Parade,
Ilkley, Yorkshire and
39 Great Russell Street,
London WC1

NOTE

The following works are reproduced (original size) with permission:

1) Robert Persons, *Newes from Spayne and Holland*, 1593, from a copy in the library of Lambeth Palace, by permission of the Librarian.

References: Allison and Rogers 634; STC 22994.

2) Richard Smith, *A brief inquisition*, 1630, from a copy in the library of St. Edmund's College, Ware, by permission of the President. This copy has suffered some cropping, especially in the marginalia.

Reference: Allison and Rogers 773; not in STC.

3) Saint Bonaventure, *The Psalter of the B. Virgin Mary*, 1624, from a copy in the library of St. Edmund's College, Ware, by permission of the President.

Reference: Allison and Rogers 129; not in STC.

NEVVES
FROM SPAYNE
AND HOLLAND
CONTEYNING.

An information of Inglifh affayres in Spayne
vvith a conferrence made theruppon in Am-
fterdame of Holland.

VVritten by a Gentleman trauelour borne
in the lovv countryes, and brought vp
from a child in Ingland, vnto a Gentleman his frend and Ofte in London.

Anno, M. D. XCIII.

TO THE IN-
DIFFERENT AND
DISCRETE READER.

I Receaved great content-
ment, and thoughte my self
exceedingly gratified by an
espetiall freind of myne, vvhen
as (of late) it pleased him to có-
municate vvith me the ensuing
discours, concerning the estate,
residence, & exercises of the
Englifh nation in Spaine,
vvith other matter thereon de-
pending, together vvith a fami-
liar conference had at Amster-
dam, vvhich also concerned Englifh affaires. But beeing in
vvritten hand, & only intended
by one freind vnto an other, I
vvas sory that so notable matter

A 2   as is

as is therein deliuered, could not so redely be imparted to many, & therefore I haue presumed to put the same in print, the thing (in my opinion) right vvoorthely deseruing thesame, & I vvish that thy acceptance thereof may be ansvverable to my good meaning, vvhereby I may the sooner be enduced for thy further satisfaction, to put foorth in print also the other discours, promised in the end of this, vvhereof I do very shortly expect to haue a copy, and thus I leaue the to God, & this treatise (in the meane tyme) to thy considerate regard.

TO THE

TO THE RIGHT

WOORSHIPFVL M. N. MY GOOD

OSTE AND DEARE FREND ABIDING

IN GRACIOVS STREAT IN
LONDON.

F I haue byn fomwhat lon-
ger then you expected (my
good ofte and deare frende)
in performance of my promi-
fe made vnto you at my de-
partur from London, to returne you fpedilie aduifes from
flaunders and Spaine, of the affaires fo much
defired and recommended vnto me, no feare haue I in the world but that my pardō fhal eafily
be obteyned at your hádes who know my good
wil both to you and your country (which for diuers caufes alfo I may wel cal myne) and more
thé this, by your own experieuce you may eafilie
imagyn the letts & difficulties which trauelers
and traffiquers are wout to finde in forraynę
countries, for difpaching their bufines with in
the compaffe of their own defignments.

True it is, that after my departing from you
(which was on Michelmas day (if I forget not)
my paffage was with good fpeede to Holland,
and thence alfo with no leffe opportunitie to

A 3   Spaine,

Spaine, for that finding good occasion of imbarcation my haste, was the greater and so I ariued in Calliz of Andaluzia, by the end of Nouēber, from whence passing within two or three dayes to the porte of S. Maries (which is but one or twwo howers sayling by water as you know) I had fitt occasion to informe my selfe very particularlie of the first pointe whereof we had hard so much in Ingland, and I promised to write you the truth to witt of the publique reconciling of so many Inglish Soldiars to the Catholique Romaine faith, as were at that tyme detayned prisoners in the Gallies of Spayne, which gallies commonly for the winter tyme doe reside in this porte of S. Maries as fittest of all Spayne for that purpose to resist the incursion of the moores. And for that this was the first matter wherof you and I talked and disputed so much in Ingland vppon the vncertaine relations that Souldiers brought vs thither from Spayne, you suspecting the matter to be feigned and I thinking the contrary; I shal first assure you in this that the whole hapned as we were informed,

Nynty Inglishmen reconciled in Spayne. to witt, that aboue nyntie Inglish, partlie capteines, and officers and partlie marchaunts and commō Souldiers, who had byn very resolute a long tyme in their religion, and had oftentymes affirmed to the Adelantado their general and other Captaynes and frendes which dealt with them in that b half, that they would rather dye then relent therin, yet afterwardes vppon three or foure dayes cōference with an Inglish father

or two

or two of this side, they offered al most willingly to chainge their opinions and become catholiques, and that at such a tyme, when as they saw themselues out of al dainger if they would haue continued in the contrary, for that they had now this kings warrãt, both for their liues and liberties, and that the inquisition should in no wise touch them for their religiõ, which I doe ad to the end you may not thinke parchãce that they did it for feare, but rather of their owne free vvil and electiõ, professing themselues with teares and extended handes (as heer most crediblie it vvas tould me) that theyvvere, all most fullie satisfied, persuaded & conuinced, & consequently desired with, earnest request to be recõciled to the Catholicke Romaine fayth and church; and so they were, euery one being first confessed of all his life past, and afterward al together in solemne procession vvere caried to the great church of the port, & there hard masse together, vvith extraordinary shew of contrition and repentance for the tyme past, & masse being ended, they al receaued the holy Sacrament of the aulter most deuoutly, & the Adelatado with diuers other noble men kinghts and Captaines were communicated with them, for their comfort and deuotion: & that ended, the Adelantado (vvho is a most noble and honorable gentleman and affected excedingly to the Catholiques of your nation) had them all home to his owne house, & gaue them a ryall dinner himselfe seruing them at the table, with *Don Iuan de Padilla* his eldest

A dinner made to the Inglish cõuerted.

his eldeſt ſonne, and heir, the marques of Montes Claros his nephew, *Don Iuan de Porto Carera* brother to the Earle of Palma his other nephew, *Don Iuan de Robles, Don Pedro de Acumnia,* & many other great men, vvho al did this honor to your nation that day, for ioy to ſee them ſo wilingly made Catholiques, and I aſſure you that this day is one of the moſt memorableſt that euer your nation hath had in theſe partes, and vvilbe remembred in the porte of S. Maries and places there about, for long tyme.

A conſideration vppon the former cõuerſion. By al which you may ſee, if you wil ſmy good Sir) that it is true vvhich ſo offen I haue vrged vnto you and others not greatly learned, who are ſo determinate in your opinions without knowing the groundes wheron you ſtãd, or at leaſt not thoſe vvherin others doe founde them ſelues, or vvhat truly may be ſaid vvithout heare of cõtentiõ, for the one or agaynſt the other, ſo if (I ſaie) you would be content but only to heare and examine the matter and confer with ſome learned of the other ſide vvith indifferent deſire to know the truth & to acknowledge it when in conſcience you ſhould diſcouer the ſame; it vveare an eaſie matter to come to that vnion ſo much deſired, as many haue dõne, which ſincerly and vvith chriſtian diſpoſition before mẽtioned haue bine content to treate of this affaire. but others as your ſelfe and ſome freinds of ours ther with you are vvont to apprehend ſo vehementlie euery new opinon that you fall on, as ther is no reaſon or argument, may be hard to
the con-

the contrary & fo no maruaile though you remaine ftill with your owne perfwafions. And
fo much by this occafion againft you good Sir,
and novv to the courfe of my narration againe.

From the porte of S. Maries I vvent to Siuil
agaynft Chriftmas and in the vvay I paffed by
S. Lucars vvher I founde the Inglifh Church
of S. George appartayniug in tymes paft vnto
the Inglifh marchantes (vvhich is an other
poynte alfo vvherof you defired to be informed)
deliuered vp into the handes of Inglifh Seminary priefts, together vvith all the houfes,
groundes, and other emoluments belonging
therunto, and it feemeth that the place hath
gotten much by this chainge, for that the fame
church (which I knevv fome yeares ago while
it was in your marchâts handes) much in decay,
is now very vvel repaired and kept in good order, and fayre habitation is in buylding about
it, vvhich they fay fhal ferue, not only for the
prieftes to lye therin, but alfo for the marchantes of the Inglifh nation, to make ther affembly
vvhen occafion is offred, and to thefe buyldings
and reparations not only the Duke of Medina
Sidonia Lord of the towne, and the Cardinal of
Siuil metropolitan of the place, doe giue their
fauours and affiftáce for the recouery of all fuch
commodityes as euer belonged to that Church
and houfe, but the King alfo himfelfe who befides other fauours gaue them two thoufand
Crownes in money tovvards the faid buylding
this yeare paft, and fo it is like to be one of the
fayreft

The In-
glifh houfe and
Church of
S. George
in S. Lu-
cars.

fayreſt houſes and churches that is in the vvhole
city of S. Lucars.

Reſidēces
of Ingliſh
Prieſts in
Liſbon &
in the por
te of S.
Maries. This houſe is to ſerue principally for a reſi-
dence of Ingliſh Prieſts as I haue ſaid, and there
is a Doctor of diuinity of your nation prouoſt
therof at this preſent , and there end is as I am
informed not only to keepe vp and ſerue that
houſe and Church, but alſo to intertaine ſuch
Ingliſh , as paſſe in and out to the Seminaries.
For vvhich cauſe alſo the Duke of Medina Celi
lord of the porte of S. Maries is about to erect
au other reſidēce like to this in that his tovvne;
and an other ther is alredy erected in Liſbone, &
an Ingliſh graue Prieſt. Superiour therof vvith
great probability to haue a Seminary alſo and
colledge of Ingliſh ſtudents in that city ſhort-
ly; as alredy ther is one of Iriſhmen and an
other of the ſame nation in Salamanca ſtirred vp
therunto by the example of the Ingliſh.

The In-
gliſh hou
ſe and
Seminary
in Siuill. But to paſſe forwards in my iourney I arriued
about Chriſtmas at Siuil vvher I found a good-
ly Ingliſh Seminarie newly begone & brought
to ſuch perfection as in two monethes only ther
weare almoſt fiftie perſons in the ſame , and the
ſaid Colledg is placed in the middeſt and beſt
ſituation of all the towne, and ſo vvel ſetled and
prouided for euery vvay as if they had byn ther
many yeares: for that the good vvil and affection
of the people toward them, is exceeding greate,
and they ſeeme to be rauiſhed as it vvere vvith
a kinde of admiration of them , to ſee ſo many
Ingliſh tender youthes, al bred and borne in
this

this Queenes reigne, and yet so forvvard and feruent in this their religion, as to offer them-selues to al kinde of difficulties, afflictions and perils for the same: for such is the profession cōmonly of al these youthes, and to confesse the truth it gaue me also incredible admiration to talke with them in that point, and surely it seemeth a spirit different from al other nations and men in thes dayes, and must needes procede of an higher influence then flesh and blood or vvordlie pollecy or persvvasion, if I be not de-ceaued.

I vvas present at certanie feastes and excerci-fes of learning vvhich these yong men made vp-pon certaine daies in this their new colledge be-fore, *Don Rodrigo de Castro*, the Cardinal & Arch-bishop of that citie, vvho estemeth himself & his house (vvhich is very honorable and of the most auncienteft Grandes of Spayne) to be discended of your old Dukes of Lācaster, as also before the vvhole vniuersity and cleargie of Siuil, and be-fore the Gouernour and noble men of the same, vvho flocked thither in so great numbers vppon the brute of Catholique Inglishmen, as it vvas of force to hold the said excercises in the greater courte of the said colledge, but yet adorned very decetly for that purpose, & suerlie the excercises feemed to be done vvith general approbation or rather admiration of al men.

The one Dayes'excercise vvere disputations before and after dinner, vppon Conclusions drawne out of al diuinity, the learnedest men of
al that

al that city and vniuerfity repayring thither to
difpute vvith the Inglifh prieftes that defended
the conclufions.

Excerci-
fes of ler-
ning by
the In-
glifh in
Siuil. An other day vvas the feaft of S. Thomas of
Canterbery celebrated vvith great folemnity &
exceding much concourfe of al principal people
of that city, the Cardinal and fome other great
perfonages vvere intertayned vvith orations and
fpeches in Latine, at their firft entrance, vntil the
maffe began, the church and court therunto ad-
ioned, vvere addreffed and hanged vvith gieate
ftore of rich clothes, & thereppon mnch variety
of poemes and learned inuentions in Latin,
Greeke, Hebrue, Frèch, Spanifh, Italian, & other
languages vvherein thefe ftudents feme to haue
much vfe and fkil, fome in the one, and fome in
the other. The maffe vvas fonge with great folé-
nity, by one *Don Alonfo de Columna*, brother to the
general of the Kings galleons. Two Sermonos
vvere made by two Inglifh fcollers, the one in
Latine, towards the midle of maffe, after the
gofpel which indured about au houre, the other
in fpanifh after the maffe vvas done, which Was
fomvvhat fhorter, but I can affure you that
both the preachers acquitted thefelues in fuch
order, as they gaue vvonderful contentement &
drew many teares from the hearers, as I can be
witnes, and I muft nedes confeffe, alfo that al
beit I be not harde to perfuade my felfe vvel of
Inglifh men as you may geffe yet eafely fhould
I not haue beleued that your countrymé could
fo vvel haue framed themfelues, to giue fatisfa-
ction in

ćtion in other countryes if I had not seene and hard this my selfe, though alwaies I haue knowne Inglish mens talents and abilityes to be great, vvherunto soeuer they list to apply themselues.

Thus passed that day vvhich vvas the 29. of December and fift day of Christmas, vvherin S. Thomas vvas slayn in his owne Church of caterbury, as you know, King Henry the secod being then in Normandy, but yet he vvas pre-sumed to be the cause and occasion of this fact, though himselfe denied his intentio thereunto al his life after. but the vniuersal Church of Christendome condemned him therin, and be-gan presently to celebrate this feast, euery yeare by publique authority, as of a martyr, and ap-poynted the gospel for the masse of thys day, to be taken out of the 10. of S. Iohn, vvher Christ setteth downe the difference betwene the good shepheard & the bad, for that the bad shepheard and hireling runeth avvay vvhen he seeth the vvolfe comming to deuoure his sheep, but the true shepheard stayeth & sticketh to the defen-ce of his sheep, and offreth his life for the same if need be, as our Sauiour sayeth in thes wordes, *Bonus Pastor animam suam dat pro onibus suis* the good Pastor giueth his life for his sheep.

These vvordes the first of the tvvo scollers that preached in Latin, tooke for his theame, & applyed them to the present feast of S. Thomas, vvhich he said did appertaine to euery seueral sort and degree of people there present, and that for diuers

S. Tho-mas of Caterbury his feast in Siuil.

for diuers perticular reafons vvhich he touched
in his preface, vvhich preface for that it fetteth
foorth the great variety of honorable perfonages
that vvere at his fermon, I fhall not omit to put
it downe here vvord for vvord as it vvas vttred
& that alfo in Latine, although yon be no great
Latinift, but I fhal take payn alfo to put the
fame in Inglifh. Thus then he began vvith as
much commelynes, grace of fpeach, and feruour
of fpirit, as euer I remembre to haue hard any
man in my life before.

THE BEGINNING OF
the Latine Sermon.

DIcturus hodie de præclarißimo Ecclefiæ Catholicæ
lumine diuo Thoma Cantuarienfi (Illuftrißime
Cardinalis, clarißimique auditores) illud fæpe mecum ad
folatium cogitare foleo, nihil me dicturum in hac tanta
frequētia, quod ad omnes ferè non pertineat; cum nemo
fortaffe fit ex vniuerfa hac nobilißimaque hominum co-
rona, qui aliquid fuum in gloriofißimo hoc Dei feruo nō
agnofcat. Dicturus enim fum de ciue apud ciues, de fe-
natore apud fenatores, de iudice apud iudices, de regni
cancellario apud conciliorum præfides; de religiou ffer-
tore, apud religionis vindices, de Paftore vigilantißimo,
apud animarum duces: de regularis vitæ profeffore, apud
regularis vitæ obferuātißimos: de Archiepifcopo apud ar-
chipræfulem: de vniuerfi regni primate apud vniuerfalis
Ecclefiæ purpuratum antiftitem : de martyre denique,
apud martyrij cupidos, fi Dominus eos dignos inuenerit.
                                                        Itaque

6

Itaque cum omnium partes in præsenti celebritate repe-
riantur, quid ni omnium quoque votis, omniumque pre-
cibus ad communem omnium Dominum recurramus, vt
dicentem me hodierno die, vel narrantem, vel perorantem
vel supplicantem, vel lamentantem etiam, & comploran-
tem, (si id vel temporum vel rerum Anglicanarum ne-
cessitas postulabit) diuina sua gratia comitari dignetur?
& in primis beatissimam eius matrem (quam summa
semper religione Archiepiscopus Thomas venerabatur)
omni contentione imploremus, vt dexteram porrigat di-
centi, & fluentem orationis meæ cursum ad filij sui glo-
riam pientissime dirigat.

In Inglish thus.

Hauing to speake this day (most excellent &
renowmed Cardinall, and you the rest most honorable auditors) of that right famous and noble light of Christs catholique church S. Thomas of Canterbury one point am I well to remember for my comfort that I shall speak
nothing this day in this noble audience which
in some sorte pertayneth not to all that are present, seing there is scarse any man in my opinion
in this most ample & honorable assembly which
may not acknowledge some parte of his estate
calling or condition, to be resembled in this
most glorious seruant of our Sauiour

For if you consider wel, my speech must be
of a citizen vnto cityzens, of a Senator vnto se-
nators, of a iudge vnto iudges, of a head and
Chancelor of a kingdome vnto the heades and
presidents of honorable counsels, of a defendor

1. Citizens
2. Coûcelours.
3. Iudges.
4. Presidentes of concelles

B   of religion,

5. Iquisitores.
6. Pastors & preachers.
7. monkes & friers.
8. Archbishopes
Cardinales.
9. Inglish schollers dedicated to martyrdom.

of religion, vnto them that by office do protect religion; of a vigilant pastor vnto those that are Captaines in guyding soules, of him that professed reguler life, vnto such as are most obseruant of regular austerity, of an archbishop to an archprelate, of the primate of an vniuersal kingdome, to a Cardinal of Chrifts vniuersal church, and finally of a maityr to them that are desirous of martyrdome, if god shal finde them worthy of so great a dignity, wherfore seing al that are prefent haue there parts in this holy celebrity; what remayneth but that with the prayers of al we make recourse to him, that is master and Lord of al, befeching his diuine maieftie to accompany me this day vvith his holy grace, while I in this sermon shal recount, declare, perfuade, implore, cry out, complaine or weepe in your prefence, according as the confideration of thefe tymes or the most afflicted state of our defolate country shal enforce me to do. And first of al, let vs begin with our humble recourse vnto his glorious mother the blessed virgin Marie, whom S. Thomas euer honored with fpecial deuotion, defiring her vvith al inftance to affift me in this action for the directing the courfe of this my fpech, vnto the honor & glory of her fonne, our Sauiour.

This vvas the entrance vnto his fermon which he profecuted after with fuch feruour of fpirit, choife of good vvords and tender matter, as no man I thinke paffed vvithout
his part

his part of teares, as before I tould you, and
fuerly if it were not ouer louge I would send
you the whole sermon, as perhaps I may when
it cometh forth in print, as I think it wil,
for I haue hard diuers say they would procure
it, but for me at this tyme it shalbe enough
to haue repeted this beginning, and to adioyn
therunto (for that it semeth to me very excellent and effectuous) the very last part and
conclusion of al which he added in few wordes, about the martyrdom of sainct Thomas,
after he had vttred many notable thinges of
his life, and especially of his great austerity
in fasting, praying, vvearing of heare cloth,
chastening of his body, and other such afflictions of his flesh, which this blessed seruant of god (by testimony of them that liued with him, and haue vvritten his life)
did vse, both at home and in his banishment.
After al which this preacher brought in this co-
clusion, turning his spech to the rest of his fel-
loes the Inglish schollers there present.

THE CONCLV-
SION OF THE
SERMON.

Atque hæc dicta sint, vt hinc etiā intelligamus (fratres mei charißimi) quæ vita martyrium antece-
dere debeat; quantoque disciplina ac sanctitatis studio,
B 2   hoc sum-

hoc summum in terris bonum, à Domino sit comparandum. Thomæ verò pro hac singulari vi'æ præstantia, non est mirum si singulare quoque genus martyrij concessum fuerit; de quo cum iam mihi ingrediendam esset, vt pro rei dignitate nonnulla dicerem; video me exclusum tempore, vt ne facti quidem narrandi locus detur. Sit igitur satis vno quasi verbo summatim quæ sequutur perstrinxisse: Henricum scilicet, ficta pace Thomam in Angliam post septem annorum exilium reuocasse: quo cum venisset, & sedi suæ restitutus fuisset, nouas calumnias statim excogitatas, veteres inimicitias resuscitatas esse: Regi in Normandia degenti, verba quædam per iracundiam excidisse, quibus gratum ei putabatur fore, si vir Dei de medio tolleretur: aduolasse statim in Angliam aulicos quosdam è regia familia, qui his ipsis festis natalitijs saluatoris, Cantuariam ruentes, virum Dei, nec fugientem, nec repugnantem, nec se defendentem cum posset, nec fores claudi sinentem, sed orantem & ante altare in genua procumbentem, gladijs nefandis (proh facinus) transuerberasse. Testis est qui adfuit, qui vidit, qui historiam scripsit, qui martyrem Christi vlnis amplexus, brachium in certamine amisit, amputatum ab homicidis: testis (inquam est) Thomam in martyrio ne gemitum quidem edidisse, nec in quatuor gladiorum ictibus qui capiti eius inferebantur, vnquam manus aut brachia sustulisse, (quod homines naturæ ductu & consuetudine facere solent) vt caput tueretur, sed hæc tantum verba aliquoties ingeminasse: Pro Christo Domino & ecclesia libenter morior. O virum admirabilem, ô vocem diuinam: videte (fratres mei) ducem præstantissimū viæ vitæque nostræ, videte magistrum intuemini præcursorem. Pro Christo Domino (inquit) & Ecclesia
libenter

libenter morior. *quæ vox fortior? quæ sanctior? quæ*
præsule Christiano dignior? quæ vox Deo ad gloriam,
Angelis ad lætitiam, inimicis ad confusionem, dæmonibus
ad terrorem, nobis ad imitationem, omnibus ad exemplũ,
ipſi martyri ad triumphum cogitari potuit illuſtrior: libenter (*inquit*) morior : *& quidni libenter Thoma,*
cum mors pro Chriſto ſumpta. non ſit mors, ſed initium
potius vitæ, arrha regni, ſigillum gloriæ, porta æternitatis,
& beatitudinis complementum ? ô ſanguinem benè im-
penſum qui pro Chriſto impenditur. quidni excitemur
(fratres mei) quid ni animemur hoc exemplo: vidimus la-
bores huius martyris. breues illos quidem: ſed gloriam
ſempiternam, & gloriam quidem, quæ vera gloria eſt,
qua ille iam plus quam quadringentis annis in cælis frui-
tur, nondum vidimus. has vmbras gloriæ, quæ in terris
habentur, vidimus Thomæ mirabiliter multiplicatas, glo-
riã nimirũ miraculorũ, gloriã ſepulchri, gloriã deuotio-
nis, & concurſus omnium gentiũ: ſed inter cætera omnia,
nihil ei iam glorioſum in hoc mundo accidit, quàm quod
perſecutorem ſuum Henricum, virtute cæleſti ad tantam
pœnitentiæ humilitatem adegerit, vt nudis pedibus gemi-
bundus ad ſepulchrum eius venerit & inſinitis effuſis la-
chrymis, gemitus, ſuſpiria, & lamenta ediderit, humi etiã
proſtratus, veniam petierit a ſancto Martyre, & pœniten-
tiam ab epiſcopo pro delicto: denique poſt integram nocte̅
vigilijs, & verberibus trãſactam, humo nuda reſidens,
omnis ad ſui commiſerationem, tanto ſpectaculo commo-
uit. Quæ maior gloria? Quæ martyris vis diuinior?

O Domine Ieſu, *vita virtuſque martyrum, vtinam*
placitum eſſet in oculis tuis, hanc gratiam perſecutoribus
quoque noſtris Anglicanis facere, vt ad te conuertantur,
& quod Henrico conceſsiſti vnius Thomæ martyris exo-
B 3 *ratus pre-*

ratus precibus, id Henrici filiæ concedas, plusquam centum testium tuorum ab illa occisorum placatus intercessione. O quàm læti ageremus tibi gratias de hoc beneficio? quam sollicite laudes tuas vbique decantaremus? verum si iustitiæ tuæ seueritas hoc forte non permittat, humiliter tamen te obsecramus, vt vires saltem nobis tribuas ad præliandum prælia tua in hoc agone quem nobis proposuisti, ita vt neque vitæ cupiditas à certamine, neque metus à periculis, neque ignauia à labore nos vnquam retardet: sed omnia impendentes in tuam gloriam, patriæque salutem, superimpendamus etiam nosmetipsos si opus fuerit, vt sic aliquo modo respondeamus vocationi nostræ & infinitis beneficijs à te acceptis: de quibus gloria tibi & gratulatio & gratiarum actio in æternum.

Thus was his ending, which in your language may thus I thinke in parte be expressed though not perhaps al thing so effectually as in the latine it runeth.

A good life is needfull before martyrdō. These things of S. Thomas his great austeriti in life, I haue recouted (deare brethern & countrimen) to the end that therby also we may vnderstand partly, what manner of life, ought to goe before martyrdome, and with how great indenour of discipline and holynes, this supreme benifit and priuilege to be a martyre is to be procured at Gods handes here vppon earth: and for that S. Thomas did excell in this kynde of holynes, (as now I haue declared) no maruail if accoiding to the excellency of life, so excellent a kind of death vvas graunted him

also of

alſo. Of which ſacred death and martyrdom,
wheras now I would begin to ſay ſomwhat,
I ſee my ſelfe ſo ſtrayghtned in tyme, as there
is not ſpace to recount the very fact, wherfore
let it be ſufficient to touch the reſt that followeth in one worde, to witt that king Henry
after al theſe troobles, made feigned peace with
the good Archbiſhop, and reſtored him to
his country and Sea of Caunterbury agayne,
after he had bine ſeuen yeares abroad in ba-
niſhment ; vvhere he was no ſooner aryved,
but preſently nevv quarels and calumniations
vvere deuiſed and rayſed agaynſt him agayne;
and thervppon the king being then in Normandy incenſed with coller, ſpake in his rage, certaine doubtfull woords, vvherby it vvas
conceaued that it ſhould be gratful vnto him,
if the archbiſhop by violence vvere made
away: by which conceat, certayn wicked cour-
tiors of his owne family, departing from thence
and ruſhing into Canterbury, euen in this fe-
ſtiual dayes of holy Chriſtmas good hearers,
ſet vppon this ſeruant of god, who nether fled
nor refiſted, nor defended himſelfe as he might, The man
nor ſuffred the dores of the Church to be ner of
ſhutt: but praying and caſting himſelfe befo- S. Tho-
re the high alter, on his knees, ſuffred him- mas mar
ſelfe moſt innocently to be ſlaine by wicked tyrdom.
taytifes. Witnes wherof, is he among others,
that vvas preſent when the act vvas done, he
that ſavv it vvith owne eyes, he that vvrote the
ſtory, he that held the bleſſed martyr in his

armes,

armes, vvhile he vvas flayne, and had his ovvne arme cutt of by the murtherers for his labour.

This man I faie is witnesse vnder his owne hand vvriting, how that S. Thomas in al his martydome, neuer gaue out fo much as one grone or figh, nor in fower blovves ftryken at his head, wherby his braynes were beaten on the pauement, he neuer fo much as lifted vp his handes or armes to defend his head (as men by natural inftinct in fuch cafes are wont to doe) but only repeated once or tvvife thefe wordes, *I dye moft willingly for Chrift and for his Church.* O admirable man, o heauenly fpeach, behold heere (my louing brethren of this colledg) behold here a moft excellent Captaine of this our life and courfe that we are to follow: behold our mafter, behold our forerrunner, what fpech more valiant, what voice more holy? what wordes more vvorthy of a Chriftian prelat? what fentence more excellent can be imagined, eyther to the glory of god, or to the ioy of angels, or to the terror of diuels, or to the confufion of his enymies, or for our imitation, or for the example of al pofterity, or for the edification of the vniuerfal world, or for the endles triumph of this martyr himfelfe.

I die mofte willingly (fayeth he) *for Chrift and his Church* o holy martyr, o blefled Thomas, thow haft great reafon to die willingly in fuch a caufe, for that death fuffred for Chrift thy mafter, is no death at al, but rather a beginning of a lóger life, an

life, an earnest peny of an euerlasting kingdom, a seale of glory, a gate of eternity, & the very complement of al felicity. O blood vvel spent that is spent for Christ, why should not vve stir vp our selues (deare bretheren) why should not we be animated and inflamed vvith this example? vve haue seene the labores and toyles of this martyr, though great, yet short and sone ended, but his glory is euerlasting. And yet the true glory which he hath euioyed novv aboue foure hundreth yeares in heauen, which only indeede is to be called glory, vve haue not yet seene. These shadovves only of glory, vvhich on earth are to be seene, we haue beheld most wonderfuly multiplied vnto S. Thomas: I meane (good hearers) the glory vppon earth of his infinite miracles, the glory of his Sepulcre, throughout al Christendom, the glory of the vniuersal concourse and deuotion of al nations vnto him. but among al other glories and glorious accidents happned vnto him, no one thing was euer more glorious or admirable, then that soone after his death, by vertue from heauen, he procured to King Henry his persecutor such grace and humility of repentance, as that he came barefooted vvith many sighes and sobbes vnto his tombe, and ther prostrating himselfe vppon the ground vvith fluds of teares, asked pardõ of the blessed martyr and penance of the Bishop for his offences, and so after a vvhole night spent in vvatching prayer and beating of him selfe, and lying vppon the bare ground he departed, leauing al the lokers

B 5   ou most

on most deeply moued with his harty repentance, what greater glory, what more heauenly force of a Christian martyr then this?

O Lord Iesu, vvhich arte the life and vertue of al martyrs would it might please thy diuine maiestie and infinite mercy to giue this grace also to our Inglish persecutors, vvherby they vvould repent and turne vnto thee: and that vvhich thow didest graunt vnto king Henry by the only prayer of thy martyr sainct Thomas, that his sinnes might be forgiuen, thow wouldest graunt the same vnto king Henryes daughter at the intercession of aboue an hundreth of thy glorious martyrs whom she hath slayne, that she might not perish: O how ioyful should we render thankes vnto thee, for this so singuler and desired a benefite! oh how chearefull should we singe euery where thy prayses for the same, But if perhaps the seuerity of thy iustice, do not permitt this, yet most humbly we do beseech thee, to giue vnto vs thy vnworthy children, here present, so much strenght and heuenly fortitude, as to fight manfully and hold out chearfully in this combat which thow hast prepared for vs, so as neyther desire of life, may stay vs from this batail, nor feare of death from perill, nor slouth from labour in this thy cause, but that we bestowing our selues wholy vnto thy glory and to the saluation of our owne selues, and of our country, we may giue our soules vp also, and pay our blood in this holyvvork, if need require, and

quire, and therby in some sort be answerable
vnto our vocation, and to the infinite benifits
which of thee we haue receaued, for vvhich
both praise glory gratulation and thankes giuing be vnto thee for al eternity. Amen.

This was the end of his speach, & by this you
may imagine of what tenor the residue vvas.
The other sermon made after masse in Spanish
I vvil not repeat, for breuity sake, and for that
by this you may easely gesse the effect therof
for it vvas to giue the people a reason of so many Inglish mens comming forth of Ingland in
these dayes, what were the true causes and necessities therof, what ther vsage was at home,
what their end abroade, and what particuler
purpose and profession these youthes that cam
for study sake to Siuil had before their eyes:
In al which as there were many things of edification, compassion and tendernes in the behalfe
of these youthes, so were ther also diuers poyntes (though vttered truly with great modestie)
which pinched to the quick, and to heare them
could not but giue me exceding grief for the
many causes I haue to houour and loue your
Country as you know. and truly I imagine that
if the Queene or some of her counsayl had bine
present, it would haue moued them much, and
that perhaps to a far other sense & meaning the
you conceaue, but now things grow to further
breach and exasperation euery day, and god only
knoweth what wilbe the ende of al.

I had almost forgotten to tel you of a certaine
fayre

The effect of the se-
cond ser-
mon in
Spanish.

fayre paper set vp this day in the Inglish Colledge emongst other poemes, and lerned deuises of the schollers, which paper did represent the antithesis or contrary procedinges of tvvo King Henries of England, to witt, king Henry the second before mentioned, vvho persecuted S. Thomas of Canterbury in his life, but after repented as hath bin shewed, and king Henry the eight vvho fower hundred yeares after his death cited and condemned him and destroyed his sepulcre which the other had built vp and many kinges after him richly adorned : The deuise was witty and the paper pleasant to behold, being large and fayrely paynted to the eye, and it drew many to looke vppon it, and to take out coppyes therof and by this tyme I thinck it to be engraued and printed, and therfore in this place I wil repeate the same vnto you briefly as it stoode.

THE REPRESENTA-

tion of the tvvo persecutions by the tvvo King Henryes of Ingland agaynst S. Thomas of Canterbury.

IN the topp of the paper vvas vvritten this title *Triumphus Sancti Thomæ Cantuariensis de duobus Henricis Angliæ regibus*, which is, the triumph of S. Thomas of caterbury ouer tvvo king Henryes of Ingland.

Vnder the title are placed the tvvo king Henryes

Henryes to witt, king Henry the second on the right hand armed and angry and stoking at S. Thomas that was paynted before him, flying away and fallyng downe on his knees, and ouer the kings head is written *Henricus Secundus Angliæ Rex*, and betwene him and S. Thomas was written, *Perſequitur viuum & fugientem*, he purſueth him in his life flying from him : On the left ſide is paynted king Henry the eight very fatt and furious and S. Thomas lying before him vvith the enſignes of glory, and ouer the king is written, *Henricus octauus Angliæ Rex*, and betwene them is written, *Perſequitur mortuum & regnantem*. He purſueth him dead and rayning in heauen, and this is the firſt ranck, conteyning fouver pictures as you ſee the tvvo kings and S. Thomas tvviſe put in the middle, once aliue and then deade & glorious.

In the ſecond ranck are ſet the afore ſaid two The ſecod ranck kinges agayne and in the middle the tombe and ſepulcre of S. Thomas as it was in Caunterbury, very rich & ſumptuous, but the kings, are paynted in different manner, for king Henry the ſecond is paynted leane and repentant, barefooted kneeling on his knees, and whipping himſelfe ſeuerly before the ſaid ſepulcre, as in truth the matter paſſed, and it is written betwene the ſepulcre and him. *Ad ſepulcrum martyris pœnitentiam agit*, he did penance at the martyres tombe; but on thother ſide king Henry the eight is paynted more fatt and monſtrous them before ſweating and chaffing and in great fury digging downe the ſepulcre the sepulcre with a pickaxe and the writing is: *Sepulcrum martyris demolitur , & cineres diſsipat*: he breaketh downe the martyrs tombe and casteth abroad his aſhes into the ayer.

The third ranck.   In the third ranke are paynted vnder king Henry the second, many angels with garlands & crownes in their handes expecting him to glory and saluation, for his penance and harty amendment, and ouer ther heades is written: *Inuitat ad gloriam*, they doe inuite him to glory, and vnder king heury the eigh are paynted as many diuels with instruments of torments in their handes, and ouer their heades is written. *Expectant ad penam*, they expect him to puniſhment & betwene both, theſe in the midle is paynted Queene Elizabeth beholding sadly the one and the other example, & ouer her head is written *Elizabetha Henricorum filia*, for that ſhe is diſcended of both theſe Henryes, and the ſentēce written beneth is *E duobus elige*, chooſe which you wil of thes two.

The 4. ranck.   In the fourth, rack are placed two Ingliſh ſtudents in their Colledg garments, one on the one ſide of the paper and the other on the other, holding vp the ſaid paper, and offring each of them ſix verſes in Latin to Queene Elizabeth for explication of their meaning in this repreſentation, and ouer the verſes is written this title.

A D ELI-

AD ELIZABETHAM

Angliæ Reginam Alumni Collegij An-
glicani Hispalensis:

The first Scholler sayeth thus.

REgibus Henricis atauis proauisque Britannis
    Edita, & hoc ipso nomine, nata patre:
Cerne quid acciderit, bellum est vtrisque nefandum
    Cum Thoma, at dispar finis vtrique fuit.
Hic gemitu vitam tulit, iste furore gehennam,
    Quid speres, timeas, quidque sequaris habes.

The second Scholler in effect vttereth the
same sence but in other words as followeth.

Concipit Henricus scelus impium atroxque secundus,
    At scelus octauus aggrauat octagies.
In Christi famulum fremit is, furit alter, at iste
    Tetrius, hoc vitæ finis vtrique probat.
O vtinam iusto perpendas pondere vtrumque:
    Et spectes atauum, non imitere patrem.

It shal not neede that I expounde thes verses
vnto you, & much lesse that I put them into Inglish poesie seing my skill and vse therin is not
great: the somme is that they doe propone vnto
her maiestie, the acts and endes of both thes
kings hir progenitors, wishing her rather to
follow the example of king Henry the second,
that repented his sinnes, then king Henry the
eight that died in the same.

I doe not remēber any other thing that I haue,
to write vnto you about this colledg in Syuil
                                            except

except I should tel you how these schollers seme to shroude themselues very peculiarly vnder the protectiō of our blessed ladye the Queene of heauen, agaynst the persecution of your Queene of Ingland. For to this ende it semeth there custome is to meete at the church, euery day after dynner to say our ladyes letanies, besides the common letanies of the church which they vse to say after supper; and to the like ende it semeth the puting vp of our ladies picture serueth ouer there gate at the very entrance of their first courte, where two scollers are paynted kneeling before her with these fowre verses betwene them for explication of these wordes written aboue.

ANGLIA DOS MARIÆ.

INgland is the Dowry of our ladye: the reason of which woordes these schollers doe yeeld in these verses saying.

Prima dedit sceptrum conuersa Britannia nato
Virginis; hinc dicta est Anglia, dos Mariæ.
Ergo tuam repetas mater sanctißima dotem,
Quique tuo repetunt iure, tuere pia.

The sence of which verses is, that for so much as Britanie now called Inglande, was the first kingdome that wholy togeather gaue it selfe and submitted her kingly scepter vnto Christ Iesus the sonne and spouse of our lady; therfore by a certayne deuout kinde of speach, ould Inglish authors did say Ingland to be the Dowry of our ladye, which being so, these scollers in consideration that her and al other saints honor,

honor, is excluded from thence they do be-
fech hir to recouer agayne this her auncient
dowrye, and fo affift them that goe in her fonnes
name and hers to negotiat the matter, by prea-
ching and teaching and offring their blood for
regayning the fame. Further doth ther not come
to my remembrance, any other newes at this tyme to writ you out of thes pattes, of Spayne, ex- *Diuers*
cept I fhould tel you of the fundry bookes that *bookes*
I haue feene here printed of late, in diuers coun- *written*
tries againft the laft proclamation publif h ed in *the laft*
Ingland, vppon the 29. of Nouember the yeare *Inglifh*
paft of 91. agaynft Catholiques and for their *tion.* *proclama-*
fearching out and apprehenfion, which procla-
mation is fet abroade in many languages and
many bookes written agaynft the fame, printed
as I haue faid in dyuers nations, which doe make
both the thing and manner of proceeding of
your cõmon wealth in this behalfe, very odious.
Three bookes in Latine haue I feene, befides
fundry in Inglifh which I name not, the firft
was fet forth by one Ioánes Pernius in Germany, *Ioannes*
and dedicated vnto your Lord Treaforer whom *Preuius.*
he fcowreth in particuler, and by a larg and
fharpe difcours refuteth the faide proclama-
tiõ, & fetteth downe the inconueniences of this
your proceeding.

The fecond author that I haue feene is of *Andreas*
Rome and calleth himfelfe Philopatrus wherby *Philopa-*
it may perhapps be prefumed that he would fi- *trus.*
gnifie himfelfe to be a louer of his country and
he fetteth downe the whole proclamation at

C　　　　large

large word for word, in fiue partes or sections, &
aunswereth to euery particuler thinge spoken
in the same, as namely touching the pope, the
kinges of Spaine, & fraunce, the Seminaries, and
Inglish seminarie priestes both abrode and
at home, & the like, shewing al my L Tresorers
accusations and asseuerations, touching thes
poynts to be euidently false and founded commonly in playne lying, and this not only in matters of religion, but also in al other publique affayres and negotiations, which is a sore blemish
to so publique a person for the which I can af-
sure you this man giueth him many wayes such
rough hewing and vttereth so many particulers
of the present state of Ingland, and vseth so
often your owne lawes stories, and cronicles to
proue it, as it maketh all sortes of straungers
wonderfully desirous to reade it.

 The third author which I haue seene wrotte
in flaunders as it semeth, and is named *Dydimus*
Dydimus
veridicus. *Veridicus* as a man would say Thomas tell truth,
vvho being a subiect of this kinge as he preten-
deth, and both witty and eloquent and taking
vppon him principally to defend the king his
masters procedings towards Ingland, and to
refute the particuler accusations, layed agaynst
him in the proclamation, he waxeth very sharpe
many tymes not only agaynst my lord Trea-
sorer as philopater doth, but also agaynst the
whole state vvhich greaueth me to reade.

 As for example, at the begining in the 9. page
of his booke, for that my Lord Burley semed to
            bragg

bragg in his proclamation of the moſt quiet
ſtate and gouerment of your common vvealth
for 33. yeares togeather, while other common
wealthes rounde about you haue lyued in broyles; this man taketh in hand, not only to proue
that all thes broyles haue bin procured by Ingland, but alſo that Ingland it ſelfe is far of from
al condition and nature of a true quiet common
vvealth and thus he begineth.

The peace and tranquility of a kingdome or
common wealth, is not troobled only by armes
and open vvar of the publique enemie abroad
or at home, but principally and moſt daunge- „
rouſly of al other, by the diſorder and diſagre- „
ment at home of her parts and members among „
themſelues, and by the violent proceeding of „
ſuch as manage the ſame, vvhich three exam- „
ples that enſew ſhal declare.   „

That houſe cannot in very truth be ſaid to be   1.
in peace (though yet neyther vvith their ovvne „
people within, nor vvith their, neyboures with- „
out they be not at buffets) vvhere the maſter „
liueth in ſuſpition of his ſeruants the officers „
doe beat and vex the houſhould, vvher ſome „
runne avvay, ſome hide themſelues, ſome cry „
out, ſome ſcould, other complayne, vvher al is „
ful of contention, and diſputes, noe obedience
but only for feare, no reſpect but only perforce,
vvher honeſt men doe ſtarue for hunger, innocent men are afflicted, quiet men vvhipped, ſe-
ditious & trooobleſome heades doe commaunde
and exact by terror there moſt iniuſt and violent
          C 2   commande-

2. commandements. Secondly that Shipp cannot
,, be fayd to hold a good peaceable courſe though
,, the ſea be calme and vvinde in the deck, vvhere
,, the maſter from the mariners, and ſhipmen
,, from the paſſingers do diſagree, are reuiled, be-
,, ten and ſpoyled the one by the other, ther mar-
,, chandize taken, away themſelues eyther oppre-
,, ſed or flong into the ſea, the cables, ſayles, an-
,, kers and other tackling broken, or putt into cō-
,, fuſion, the ſhip defiled with blood, and loden
,, vvith dead carcaſes, and nothing ſounding
,, vvithin, but ſighes, and ſorrowe and deſolation

3. of ſuch as miſerably liue vvounded in her. And
laſt of al, that cytie cannot be ſayd to be in
peace or in any ſecurity, (though it be infeſted
yet vvith no enemye from a broad) vvhoſe go-
uernours do giue, themſelues vvholy to terror
and crueltie, do multiply priſons, fetters, gar-
des and ſpies, do make new penal lawes & abo-
liſh the olde and do inuent new taxes and im-
poſitions euery day, do ſeeke all occaſions to
pole ther people at home, & inforce them forth
to be theeues abroad, do kepe fayth with none,
do caſt in priſon, baniſh, ſpoyle, and conſume
the better ſort, pull downe the nobility, oppreſſe the cleargy & finally do put al there hope in
the feare of the people and none in ther good
wil, thus ſaueth *Didimus* agaynſt that firſt poynt
of your L. Treſorers proclamation.

And after he hath perſued many particulari-
tyes of the afflicted and dangerous preſent ſtate
of Ingland, by reaſon of the diuiſion in religion,
diſuiſion

difuinon and hatred betwene proteftants, Catholiques,and puritans, complaints and difcon-
tentments on euery fide, incertainty of fuccef-
fion vnto the crowne, pouerty of the people for
lack of trafique, breaking of marchants for the
fame caufe, burden of vnneceffary and vnpro-
fitable warres, dayly multiplying of intolerable
tributes,peftering the realme with innumerable
renegat and rebellious ftraingers, liberty of
theeues by fo long permiffion of piracy,vniuft
vvarres, diffidence & diftruft in the one towards
the other,and open domeftical diffention in euery towne parifh and particuler houfe ouer all
the land, for one caufe or other, After al this
I fay he paffeth on to compare the eftate of
Ingland with other kingdomes & common
vvealthes abroade fhewing the great hatred &
obloquie which your country is in for ftvrring
vvarres and rebellions on euery fide, but for no
one thing more, thé for fo opé dealing with the
Turke the publique enemye of al chriftian pro- ·Dealing
feffió, inuitinge & ftyrring him to turne his for- of Englâd
ces vppon Chriftendome therby to hurt the Turck.
king of Spayne,which this mã auoucketh to be
euidét,not only by the ofté embaffages letters &
prefets fent vnto this profeffed enemye of Chrifts
name,from Inglâd thes later yeares:but alfo by a
playne letter written by the Turk himfelfe about
three or fowers yeares agone, to the Queene
about this matter foone after the defeat of the
fpanifh Armada, which letter being intercepted
in Germany & printed ther both in the Latin &

germane tonges , was afterwards publifhed agayne, and inferted into an Hiftory of our tymes, fet forth by on Ionfon Doccom of fiifelande, and now agayne laid abroad, by this Didimus and the letter is vvord for vvord as followeth, for that I fuppofe you vvilbe defirous to fee it, thus then goeth the title.

The title of the Turkes lettre. HONORATÆ A DO-
mino legis chriftianæ matronæ, culmini caftitatis, inter caftiffimas fæminas populorum, qui feruiunt Iefu, &c.

In Inglifh thus.

TO the honorable matron, honored by the lord of Chriftian lavv : to her that is the hight and topp of chaftity among the moft chaft women of al people that ferue Iefus: to her that is adorned with the glory of domination & gouernment, ladie of many kingdomes, reputed of greateft, power & prayfe among the nation of Nazarens, to witt, Elizabeth Queene of Inglád to whom we wifh a moft happy and profperous-ende.

You fhal vnderftand by thes our high and emperiall lettres, directed vnto you, that your embaffador refiding in this our high and noble court, did prefent vnto the throne of our greatnes , a certayne writing of yours which informed

formed vs , how that for thes foure yeares paſt
you haue made warr vppon the king of Spaine, Informa
therby to breake and diminiſh his forces, by tions geuen to
which he is become dreadful vnto the reſt of the Turd
Chriſtian Princes, & hath determyned to make agaynſt
the kof
himſelfe lord ouer al, & monarch of the whole Spayne.
world beſides : more ouer the ſaid lettre doth
ſhew how that the ſelfe ſame king of Spayne,
hath by violéce taken away the kingdõ of Portugall from *Don Antonie* the lawful king therof,
lawfully created : moreouer that your intention
is to lett hereafter the nauigation of this king
vnto the Indians , wherby he is wont to bring
home euery yeare into ſpayne great ſtore of gold
and ſiluer, ſpices and precious ſtones, worth ma_
ny millions, by which he is become ſo rich, as
he hath commodity to moleſt and indanger al
other Princes and if he ſhould be let a lone he
would grow to be ſo powerable that at lenght
it would be hard to reſiſt him.

Vppon which conſiderations your ſaid Em- The peti.
baſſador, did make humble ſupplication vnto tion of
our greatnes, that we ſhould vouchſafe in the the Ingliſh An
beginning of this next ſpring to ſend our impe- baſſador
rial nauy vppon the ſaid King, aſſuring vs that V Villian
Harborn
he would not be able to reſiſt the ſame, for the
great ouerthrow and damage which he hath
receaued by your nauy of late : and ſeing he is
ſcarſe able to reſiſt your forces alone , no doubt
but that he would be ouercome if of many ſides
he be inuaded at one tyme which would be
greatly (as you ſay) to the commodity of al

Chriſtian

Chriſtiã Princes, as alſo of this our high courte, to which it appartayneth to take the protectiõ of ſuch as fly vnto the ſame for ſuccour (as *Don Antonio* doth, being driuen out of his kingdome by the ſaid kinge of Spaine) and therfore, that we ſhould giue him help & ſuccour, according to the cuſtome of our noble auncetours & predeceſſors of happy memory, (whoſe ſepulcres God almightie lighten) who were wõt alwayes to giue royal aſſiſtance to ſuch as were oppreſſed and came for ayde to their imperial highneſes.

The Turkes anſwere. Theſe thinges and many other did your ſaid embaſſador declare at large before our roiall throne, al vvhich vve haue vnderſtood and layd vp dilligently in our myndes, and for the preſent our anſwere is, that vvher as we haue had vvarr now many yeares in Perſia with intention to gayne that kingdom, and to ioyne it, to the reſt of our auncient Dominions, and to reueng our ſelues vppon that accurſed heretical Perſian, that holdeth the ſame : now by the grace of our great God, and by the helpe of our moſt holy prophet Mahomet, we are very nere to obteyne our purpoſe, according to our deſire, which being once done, al neceſſary prouiſion ſhalbe made out of hand for performance of thes thinges which you deſire & demaunde, aſſuring you, that if you doe cõtinew this league of frenſhip puerly and ſincerly, vvith this our high court, you ſhall finde no refuge more ſecure, nor any haue of loue & good wil more firme & ſure then this of owrs, by which no doubt al your all your warrs vvith the fpaniards fhal fuccede vnto you according vnto your defire, vnder the fhadow & protection of this our happy throne, and feing tne king of Spayne hath gotten by fraude & violéce, al that he poffeffeth, no doubt, but by the grace of god, al fuch fraudulent deceauers fhal quickly be deftroyed.

In the meane fpace we do exhort you to lefe no tyme nor occafion to do him hurt, but to be watchful and diligent, and according to the couenaunts alredy made betwene vs, that you fhew your felfe a frend to our frendes, and an enimye to our enimyes, and that you fignifie from tyme to tyme vnto this our high courr, vvhat new warres foeuer be taken in háde in thofe partes, and what you can vnderftand, concerning the King of Spaine to our and your commodity, furthermore I am, to aduertife you, that this your embaffador hauing done his duety, and fulfilled the function of his embaffie with great care & diligéce, & hauing left here in his place for his cómiffary & agent, Edward Bardon he departeth now with our licence towards your kingdome, who for his faythfnl feruice here performed deferueth no doubt to be much efteemed honored & exalted aboue others, and when he hath gotten all thofe honores & preheminenfes of you, which he deferueth, let him returne agayne prefently with your letters, or fome other principal man in his place, to be your embaffador here, and to continew this office of frendfhip betwene vs in this our high court,

The Turkes exhortation to the Q.

To be his fpie.

Commendation of the Inglifh embaffadour, by the Turke. Edvv. Bardon.

C 5   and thus

and thus much we thought good to aduertise you, by our owne soueraigne lettres and seale, which you shal giue intire credit vnto. Giuen this fiftenth of Benedicti *Rhamaram*.

Hitherto is the lettre of the greate Turke vnto your Queene, that is to say, of that greate proude and barbarous enemy of Christes holy name and religion, wheruppon this *Dydimus* doth deduce dyuers considerations of importance & consequence, as namly first of al, about religiō, and coscience, saying who would haue thought when Inglād vppō pretence of purer seruing of Christ, did first seperate it selfe in religiō frō the rest of Christian kingdomes, that it would haue come in so few yeares, to that passe, as to make recourse to Christes open enemye & persecutor, & that agaynst Christians? as also that for the hatred of some one Christian Prince, to seke to put into Christes enemyes handes, so many millions of his subiects as are in Spayne? and to put in hazard al Christendome besides.

2. The second consideration is of wisdome and pollicy tēporal, for what wisdome or pollicy in the world can ther be in this, sayeth he (though we set a side al feare of God and religion) to call so potent an enemye as the Turk is, into Spayne, or to thinke that he would be a better frend to the state and subiects of Ingland, that are Christians, then the king of Spayne, that is a Christian, or to imagin that when Spayne should be lost, Ingland could be safe, or when this ambicious tyrant should haue enthralled the spainards,

(margin note: Considerations vppon the Turkes letter.)

nards, he would fuffer the Inglifh to liue at their liberty? was not Conftantinople? was not Africa and many other realmes loft from Chriftianity by this moft diuelifh and miferable enuy, of one realme and Prince agaynft a nother.

A third confideration is of honour and repu-tation, which feemeth excedingly to be touched and diftayned by many poyntes in this lettre difcouered, for what a thing is it fayeth he, that Ingland which was wont to be a kingdome of fo great honour, nobility, and valor in kingly proceding, fhould now come to make fuch a narratió to the great Turke, as here is fet doune, by the tyrants owne letter, to witt, that the kinge of Spayne meant to make him felfe lord of al Chriftédome, and monarch of al the world; that he hath taken Portugal by violence from *Don Autonio* the lawful king, & lawfully created, vvheras al the world knoweth that the Kings title to Portugal was decided by the lawes of that kingdom it felfe, and by the approbation of the laft king Cardinal of the fame, vvho alfo pronounced *Don Antonio* for an open knowne baftard, vvhom all the nobility afterwards re-fufed and no man euer created him king, but only a few of his owne feruants and fome other of the bafer vulgar people follicited by them in Lifbone and other partes neare ther about: and yet that Ingland to the Turke fhould aduoutch him playnly for a lawful king and put out by violence, exhort the Turke to reftore him by his forces according to the cuftome of his noble
aunceftors

aunceſtors vvho are knowne to haue deuoured
ſo infinite chriſtian bloode and haue deſtroyed
ſo inumerable chriſtian eſtates wherein our Sauiour vvas longe honored and now Mahomet
is adored: that England ſhould offer concurran-
ce in this diueliſh action, and ſhould take a có-
miſſion from the Turck (as in this his letter is giuen) to be a ſpie agaynſt the reſt of chriſtianity,
and to aduertiz him of al new vvarres & aſſayres
that paſſe amonge Chriſtian Princes, & finally
to be a frend to al his frendes, and enimy to al his
enimyes, vvhich is the higheſt infamye that euer
could fal vppon any ſtate realme or kingdome
that beareth the name enſigne or profeſſion of
Chriſtian religion.

Great in-
dignitye
to Ingläd.

Thes and other contemplations hath this author vppon this matter, vvhich I paſſe ouer and
do come to tel you that beſides thes bookes and
tretiſes vvritten in Latine, I haue alſo ſeene diuers pamphlets vvritten in Ingliſh agaynſt this
proclamation no leſſe ſtinging then the other
in Latin, and al of them both of the one and
the other ſorte, tranſlated commonly into other
vulgar tonges alſo, as Spaniſh Italian french and
flemiſh, which do make the commó ſubiect of
ordinary talke in thes dayes to be of your aſſayres in euery countrey.

Father
Ribade-
neyra
agaynſt
the procli
amation
and nevv
ſtatuts.

And laſt of al, here hath come forth a booke
in Spaniſh vvritten by one father *Pedro Ribade-
neyra* a man of very great reputation in thes
kingdomes both for his learning grauity and
eloquence in this language, and this booke
conteyneth

conteyneth the ſtorye of Ingliſh affayres from
the yeare eightie and eight (vntil vvhich time
he had ſet forth the ſaid ſtory in Spaniſh before
according to the latin ſtory of the Ingliſhe
Schiſme vvritten by D. Sanders and Riſton and
other aduertiſments) and novv he continu-
eth this, euen vnto this yeare 93. And in this
ſaid ſtory he layeth forth alſo the ſaid proclamation at large, and afterwarde writeth diuers
large chapters for explication of the ſame, wher
of the one is, (as I remember) that this procla- **Cap. 1.**
mation is moſt impious and contrary to al diuine & humane lavves receaued in any chriſtian
common vvelth, eſpecially in Ingland from her
firſt conuerſion. An other chapter is, that this **Cap. 2.**
proclamation is not only impious, but alſo
foliſh and indiſcret, againſt all good pollicy
and mature wiſdome. A third is, that it is im- **Cap. 3.**
pudent and vvritten vvithout all reſpect of
ſhame, honor, or reputation of your eſtat and
nation, auontching lye vppon lye, that al the
vvorld knoweth to be lyes, vvith diuers other
ſuch chapters which he proueth at large, &
with many particulers, & in fyne concludeth,
that the penner of this proclamation would be
ſharply puniſhed in any orderly and graue
common wealth for penning it in ſuch manner, and for auoutching ſo many open imper-
tinent lyes, and euident ſlaunders vnder the
name of his ſoueraigne, though the chiefe
matter it ſelfe therin ſet downe, vvere allo-
vved and agreed vppon by publ:que authority,
at it is

as it is fuppofed that this was by your Queene
and councel there.

The two
laft Statu-
tes. Moreouer this fpanifh book layeth forth two
new ftatutes made about religion in your laft
parliament ended the 10. of Aprill of this prefent yeare, which feeme to haue come to the authors handes euen vvhiles the former parte of
this booke was a printing, the one is intituled *an
Act to retayne the Queenes fubiects in their due obedience: and the other for reftrayning of popifh recufants
to certayne places of aboude*, by the which two ftatutes and the ftrange prouifions made therein,
as alfo, by the fundry bookes fet out by authority at this very tyme agaynft the puritans, vvith
the enditméts arraynments and ftrange anfwe-
res of Barrow, Greenwod, Studly, Billet and
other Brownifts : by al thes thinges layd together (I fay) and by the acte of three entyre fub-
fides, and fix fifteenes, and tenthes exacted and
graunted, at one clapp in this parliament , for
maynteyning of warres abroade and your eftate
at home, this writter concludeth, that neuer
common welth vvas in more miferable and
dangerous plight for al kinde of miferies that
can fal to a common wealth, then Ingland is at
this day : and confequently moft far of from
that condicion of peace, tranquility and fecurity
vvhich your lord Treaforer in this late proclamation would make men to beleeue, vvheras
himfelfe muft needes (fayeth this man) fee and
know the contrary, as al men alfo abroade do,
that are of iudgment or experience, and moreouer doe

uer doe difcouer his defperat deuife of remeding the matter by maffacring and murthing al the principall catholiques vppon the fudden vvhen foeuer he fhal fee no other fhift, for that to this end playnely femeth to tend this laft ftatute of bynding al the better and richer fort of them to refide in certayne knowne places and not to departe thence further then fiue miles vnder payne of forfeting vvhat-foeuer they haue in this vvorld, vvhich is to fill Ingland full of prifons and chaynes, as the flemifh *Didimus* before infinuated: a diuife fo ftrange vppon fo great a multitude as neuer was hard of before in any free common vvealth, nor practifed (fayeth this man) eyther by Phalaris or any other moft famous tyrant. Wherunto if vve add the fecond part of the ftatute vvherby the poorer forte of catholiques are appoynted to be thruft out of the realme, fpoyled and ranfaked, of al that they haue, it maketh the barbarous defigment more euident (fayeth he) to vvitt, that thes fhalbe driuen to ftatue abroad and the others be kept for the flaughter at home, vvhen the tyme fhall ferue, but god turneth lightly (fayeth he) all fuch cruell and bloody intentions vppon the heades of the entendors and their pofterity, and fo doth he thinke that it vvill fall out vvith your lord Treaforer and his offpring and this is all that I can vvrite vnto you from thes partes.

THE

THE SECOND PARTE

of this letter, conteyning certaine confide-
rations of State vppon the former
relation.

THis that goeth before I hadd vvritten in
Spayne to send to you from thence, but afterward ther being offred a good paffage by fea,
to returne to Holland vvith certayne company
that vvould needs haue me go vvith them out
of hand, I took my papers and came hither, wher
meeting vvith diuers gentlemen, captaynes,
fchollers, and others, as wel Inglifh, Scottifh,
Irifh, & Fréch, as alfo fome Italians & Dutchmé
both of this country and high Gérmany (for al
fortes you know do meete here now) vve fel by
chaunce into talk of Ingland, and of Inglifh
affayres vppon occafion of the former bookes
publifhed in al natiós, as hath bene faid, againft
the prefent procedinge of your ftate, & namely
agaynft your laft proclamation and ftatutes,
nevvly made about religion, by which occafion
alfo I tould them vvhat I had feene, and hard in
Spayne and read vnto them the former letter &
narration vvhich I had made redy to feale vp &
fend avvay prefently vnto you by the poft, but
aftervvardes hearing diuers politique and im-
portant difcourfes (as to me they femed) vvhich
fome of thefe men made vppon this narration
of myne, and fome confiderations alfo of ftate,
as they termed them, vvorthy the noting: I
thought

thought good to stay the letter, by me for some dayes to the end I might send you also therwith the principal pointes vvhich I hard debated, and so novv I doe.

The chiefe subiect or argument of al their speech for diuers dayes meeting at an ordinary table, vvas vvhether the present gouerment of Inglish affayres, setting a side al regard of partiality to religion; vvere in it selfe and according to reason, experience and lavv of policy, to be accounted vvise and prudent, and consequently vvhether such as chiefly managed the same, and namely the lord Burley, vvere in truth a vvise mã ǒr no? in vvhich particuler though some of the company for affection to his religion, did for a tyme stand much in his defence, yet so many vvere the argumēts of the other side, as in the end they semed greatly to yeild, & to vvith nothing so much, as that the said lord had bin present but for one houre, if it had bin possible, or some other that vvere priuy to his councelles, to yeild reason of diuers points there called in question, vvhich semed scarse defensiable, not only for lack of iustice or cõscience (for that therof they said they vvould take no regard) but that euen in nature of humane vvisdome and pollycy (set downe by Machauel him selfe, or by any other of lesse conscience then he, they seemed erronions and of thes are such as hereafter do ensue.

First some of them said (though not al) that supposing that nether the Queene nor Sir William

D

The chiefe subiect of the cõference.

The first considera tiõ about chang of religion.

liam Cecil, at the death of Queene Mary had any great repugnance of conscience to follow and continew on the religion then setled in the realme, as both of them (but especially Sir William Cecil) had oftentymes protested & euer shewed by deedes during that reigne : it semed a great ouersight in reason of state to make so vniuersal a change of religion (which hath bin the cause of al difficalties and doungers since) seing that without this change the Queene and he might haue brought about, with much more security, whatsoeuer they pretended by this other meanes, and hereuppon, were brought agayne into consideratió, al those reasons and arguments of state which at that tyme Sir William Cecil & M. Bacon did or could lay before the Queene, to moue her to this change against both her owne inclination, and the opinions of the rest of her principal councellors which reasons concerning especially (as is supposed and knowne) her Maiesties affaytes with the pope, about her fathers mariage, and her legitimation, were founde by euery mans censure here present, to be but playne illusions, for that much easier should her Maiesty haue bin able to compound those affayres with the pope, if she had continewed in his religion, then by breaking from him, and for all other temporal matters, both for her owne person & the realme they had proceded (no doubt) most prosperously, and neuer come into thes brakes & breaches wherin now the whole world seeth them to be. And as for M. Cecil and Ba

cons

tons owne particuler aduancements (vvhich is
persupposed vvere principally respected in this
persuasion) there vvould not haue wanted occa-
sions enough to furder the same also in a catholique estate, as vve see by so many aduaunced &
setvp by catholique Kinges of our country in
former ages, and the two late minions Ioyous
and Pernon, exalted in our dayes to so great dignityes by the last King of france. And *Rigouez*
of a page made a Prince, and two of his sonnes
Dukes vvith diuers others to like preferments
aduanced by the king of Spayne that novvis, &
that vvith much lesse enuy, hatred and abhomi-
nation, and vvith much more security of Conti-
nuance to their families, then the greatnes of
Cecil and Bacō is like to finde, say these men, that
vvas procured by so great a conuulsion of the
vvhole common vvealth, and therfore in this
first poynte and entrance to al the rest, they are
thought to haue byn nevther vvise nor lucky,
as one day their posterity vvil testify to the
woild, & this is the first point that was discoursed of.

The second ensewing on this first, vvas, that
supposing that change of religion had byn the
best, and surest vvay for those intents that vvere
designed, to vvitt of her Maiesties state and thes
mens preferments, yet sayd most of this our conference, it had bin a matter of farr more wisdome and pollicy (seing pollicy vvas their foundation) to haue made this change to some other
religiō receaued in the vvorld abroad, and therby

The 1.cō
sideratiō
of chang
of religiō
to a diffe
rent frō
all others

to haue

to haue ioyned vvith fome other party, or to the
communion of fome other people or prince,
when they brake from that of the Catholique,
fo ftrong and general ouer al Chriftendome, rather then to fet vp a party alone, agreeing vvith
no other vvhat foeuer. As for example, if they
had councelled her Maiefty to admitt Luthers
doctrine and religion as it lyeth, and is practifed
by the followers therof they had confequently
ioyned vvith fome Princes of Germany, as nam
ly vvith the Duke of Saxony, King of *Denmarck*
and others that make profeffion of that religion.
Or if they had perfuaded her grace to haue imbraced the religion of Caluin plainly and inti-
rely as he taught and exercifed thefame, then
had they entred therby into communion and
frenfhip vvith Geneua and diuers others ftates
of Swizerland, as alfo vvith the Princes of the
religion, called the reformed in France Flanders
and Scotland, and by thes meanes, at leaft had
they gayned fome new party to be affured to our
realme, by this band and vnion of religiõ, which
is the ftrongeft and moft durable of al other.
But novv for them to put downe the old ftate
of religion that was fo vniuerfal and fo vvel bac-
ked, and in place therof to put vp a nevv of their
owne only deuife, that hath no ftay or trufty
frend at al, out of your owne realme, for that it
agreeth vvith no ftate, people, natiõ or common
vvealth chriftian befides your felues : vvas fuch
a peece of work (fay thes men) as a man may
rather wonder at the boldnes of the deuifers
                                                    them

then any way commend their iudgments considering the incōueniences that dayly do ensew
therof and must doe euery day more and more,
and is impossible in mans reason, that it can continew.

And albeit in Ingland simple people are often
told and many do beleue, that al new religions
sprong vp in thes dayes both in Germany, france,
Scotland, flaunders & at home, if they be against
the Catholiques; and namely those of Lutherás,
Caluinistes, and protestants are but one religion
in effect, for that they al doe ioyne in league and
frendship for the present, to resist the stronger,
yet that is as playne an error, and deception as if
vve should say, that the Turk, Persian, Iew and
Infidels, which do ioyne easily against the Christians when and wher they see him the stronger,
are al of one religion, or not enemyes among
themselues vvhen they see their owne state free
from danger of the other.

No re
gion ti
day agi
eth vvi
Ingland

Euen so, fareth it in this cause proposed, the
Lutheran, puritan, & protestant that haue taken
ech one his parte of the dominion which the
Catholique possessed, and yet seing him left so
strong and potent in Christendom, that euery
day he hopeth and seketh to recouer agayne the
possession that he hath lost, no maruaile though
they ioyne togeather, and wil seeme one for the
resisting of so vniuersal and dangerous an aduersary: but if you would see, how thes men would
agree or be frendes together, if once the Catholiques vvere extinguished, consider not only

their

The lu-
ans and
aluini-
es & pu
tas great
umyes. their difference in doctrine, wherby the one part
doth censure the others religiō for heretical and
damnable: but much more marke their manner
of proceding in gouerment, where eyther part
hath authority at wil: as for example, in thos
parts of Germany wher Luthers religion is esta-
blithed, is ther any vse of Caluins religion permitted? no truly, nor the professors therof so
much as tollerated to liue in that estate or to be
buryed in the same churches or church-yeards
with them, but are cast out euen into the common feilds, as people accursed, aud excommuni-
cated, wherof in particuler your Inglish marchants that lyue and trasique in Hambrough
or any other townes vnder Lutheran gouermēt
can wel beare witnes. Or if contrary-wise in Ingland or Geneua at this day, any company of
people would put vp the exercise of the Lutherā
masse, defende the real presence in the Sacramēt,
bring in the vse of paynted or carued images in
their churches, practise confession, hold three or
fower sacramēts as the Lutherās do: should they
not (think you) be pursued and punished? yes
no doubt, and that with reason, seing the state of
Ingland alloweth not this doctrine, nor practise of germayne religiou, wherby we may gather
what true accord and frenship ther is or may
be, betwene thes professions, or how thes people
would or could long liue together in vnity if
they had no common aduersiry.

And this of the Lutheran and reformed religiō so called in those parts of Germany, wher it
is receaued

is receaued: But if we confider the other party of reformed or new religiõ planted by Caluin and Beza in Geneua, France, Flaunders and Scotland, albeit the ftate of Inglãd do follow more points therof in doctrin then of the other before named Lutheran: yet how many and great irrecõciliable differences ther be, is abundantly fet forth in the multitude of bookes written of late the one agaynft the other, & efpecially by that fet out now prefently by order and authority of the bifhops intituled. *A furuay of the pretended holy difcipline*, wherin the puritans or fincere Caluinifts doctrine is detefted difcredited and made heretical, and feditions, yea Caluin and Beza themfelues much difgraced and impugned. Wherunto, if we go add the blood of fuch as lately they haue put to death in Ingland, for defending of this doctrine, & the others refolution to fuffer the fame: we may eafely fee what would become of thes two partes if things went to their owne willes, to witt, that eyther the puritan had fo ful power to reuenge himfelfe of the proteftant by fword, as he defyeth him in worde, or that the proteftant were fo free from fufpition and danger of the catholique, as he had leafure to extirpat the puritan as he defireth.

The lyke ts vvritten by one Sutlif.

Barovv grene vvood, Penry.

By this then do we fee euidently fayed thes mẽ, that the particuler choife & forme of religiõ which Sir William Cecil & M. Bacõ mad & perfuaded the Queen vnto at the beginning, was no wife or confiderate choife: for albeit it femed

D 4   at that

at that tyme, to ferue fitly their turnes for to put downe the old, and bring al matters into their owne handes, to place new bifhops, Deanes, Archdeacons and other like dignityes vnder the name of the Queene: yet was it moſt dangerous and preiudicial to the weal publique, in that it was peculiar, folitary and differet from al other, as hath bin declared, and confequently muſt needs expect a perpetual warr and contradictiō, and that, not only at the catholiques handes, but much more and fharper at the other two parties aboue named, if the catholique party could be extinguiſhed, fo as the labetinth of Inglifh ſtate and religion, feemeth hereby to be inextricable, and much approued was the faying of S. Chriſtopher Hatton late chauncelor, to a certayne fecret frende of his a lyttle before his death, that the clew twyned vp by thes deuifes in Ingland, was fo Intanged, as no man poſſibly could vntwiſt the fame but by breaking al in peces, which he fpake to the great grief both of himfelfe and him that heard it.

S. Chriſto phor Hatto slaying.

A third confidera tio of the manner of procee-ding by cōputilo in matters of religiō.

A third confideration was of the manner of procceding to hould vp and fett forwards this forme of religion, chofen for Ingland: in which poynte alfo thes men founde much defect of fore fight and pollicy in thes that were the firſt fitters vp therof: for if her maieſty had bin perfwaded at the begining, to haue followed the courfe of Germayne ſtates and Princes, which was to giue liberty of confcience to al, and to preſſe none by violent meanes, to be of their religion,

ligion, but only to inuite them with rewards of preferment : it is very like that matters had paffed as quietly this day in Ingland as they do in Germany, where al are quiet, and the princes safe, and little contradictions or falling out for fuch affayres. And feing that Inglifh men do come of Germayne race, it may be they would haue followed them in this poynt alfo, but howfoeuer that be, moft likely it is that matters had neuer come to thofe open broyles, hatreds and mortal enimyties that now they are come vnto in Ingland : for men being not preffed, many would haue had little care of being zelous or heddy on eyther part: & preferment only would haue moued infinite people to follow that vherby they might haue profited : and others not ftinged or compelled to the cótrary, would haue remayned doubtful, but yet quiet in their confultations, vhat way to follow, and fo fhould her Maiefty haue bin ferued of al, and hated of none, and aduauncments sufficient would haue remayned for al fuch as would haue bin forward in that her Maiefty had moft fauored.

But now by this other courfe, that hath bin taken, of turmoyling, tormenting, and beating men to their religion, the ftate is growne to be both odious a broad, and dangerous at home, and not durable. Firft, for that as the poet fayeth. *Nitimur inuetitum semper*, mans natural inclination, is to efteeme and defire that which is denyed him, and to reiect that, which is thruft vppon him by violéce. But yet in no one thinge

D 5   fo much

so much is this seene, as in matters of religion, which of al other affayres, is the poynt that most requireth liberty, both of iudgment and will, & least beareth the force of strayning: and so we see by experience, that her Maiesty at the beginning, entering and raigning for some yeares with mildnes, found no difficulty, (to speak of) on any part though at her entráce the whole realme was, settled in an other religió. but now after twenty yeares pressing men with restraints, imprisonments, losse of goodes and liues, the number is founde euery day more greater of them, that openly make resistance, and do lesse respect and reuerence both prince law and gouuermét: and so euery day wilbe more and more, both of Catholiques and puritans for the reasons afore said. Which thing certayne pollitick councellors of, Iulian the Emperor surnamed the Apostata obseruing by experiéce of al the rigorous courses of former Emperors before hym, they persuaded him to change that course of forcing, into alluring, and so he did, and wrought more effect in few yeares by that meanes, then the other had done by the contrary in many, and would (no doubt) haue done much more, if his life and reigne had not bin so short.

An obiection. To this discourse said one of the company, if this be so, how then do catholiques vse rigor in punishing them that are not of there religion, and do preuaile therin, as we see by experience of Spayne and other countryes, wherofté tymes thes new religions beginning to budd vp haue
bin kept

bin kept downe and vtterly extinguished by punishment.

To this answered an other saying, they wil The an-
sweare. saye that the cause of this is the truth of their
religion, and the falshood of the other, & that
it is peculiar to their religion, by promise of
Christ, to endure for euer, and triumph ouer al
sects: but for that this is not graunted by al but
remayneth in dispute, (I wil quoth he) yeald an
euident difference heerof in pollicy and reason,
which is, that Catholique Princes which by force and punishment, haue extinguished other
religions, and sects that began to spring vp in
there realmes, did take thos new blossomes at
the begining whiles they were yet grene, and
not wel setled and their followers not many, &
so I do confesse that all religions may be rooted
out, sauing only the trew which Christ himselfe
defendeth, and so many do thinke that if Char-
les the Emperor had apprehended Luther at his
first seing him in *Augusta*, (as many of his counsel
perswaded him) he had crushed perhapps his
doctrine in the very kyrnel, and the like may be
said of Caluin and Beza, as also perchaunce of
the puritans in Ingland if rigor had bin vsed towards them at their first rising: though this last
of the Puritans be very doubtful, for that their
foundation being (as after shalbe shewed) the
very doctrine it self that by publique authority is
set forth, taught, and maynteyned now in Ingland: it must needes continually rise out of the
same, as the heate frō the fyer so as it is impossible to

ble to nourish the one & extinguish the other.

Catholiques not eafely extinguifhed. As for the Catholiques in Ingland, the reafon is far different, for they being no new beginers but old poffeffors of the realme, they vvere fo many at her Maieftyes firft entraunce to the crowne, as they could not wel be al extinguifhed together, except the land fhould haue bin left waft, nor can be eafely at this day exringuifhed by force in any reafon of ftate or probability that I can fee: for I do not comprehende thofe only by this name, which are recufants and dif-couer thefelues vnto the world (for thofe might eafely perhapps be made away as many do fu-fpect is meant by the late ftatute of reftrayning them to certayne places) but much more do I vnderftad by this people thofe alfo, who goe not fo far forwardes as to difcouer their religion (at leaft wife to put themfelues within danger of lawes) and yet in mynde, wil, and iudgement, are they nothing behinde the reft, yea fo much the more feruent inwardly, agaynft the ftate, by how much more they are forced by feare to dif-femble outwardly their iudgements, and keep in their affections, and thes are alfo of two fortes, the one knowne or fufpected, though nothing cã be layed agaynft thẽ by law, but the other not knowne nor fufpected at al, but of good autho-rity in the realme, and fo much the more dange-rous when occafion fhalbe offred.

  Agaynft, al thes then, what doth the courfe of feuerity preuayle? thofe few that are knowne re-cufants may be vexed and toffed, as they haue bin thes

bin thes later yeares, and some particuler courtyer may be aduanced by begging their goodes
and landes, but vvhat is this to the common
wealth?none or few of them are conuerted:ther
number groweth euery day rather then demi-
nisheth, and if any do or shal yeald to goe to the
church, what is gayned therby? they change
not in iudgment, nor come vvith their hartes,
but vvith their bodyes or tong only, their inward auersion is so much the more increased
towards the state, by how much more violent
this outward compulsion is: and in the meane
space their frendes and kynred are more exasperated,their fellow catholiques not yet recusants
alienated:the people seing their afflictions more
moued to compassion towards them, forrayne
princes more egged to take their partes, what
then in the end is like to come of this.

And if you put thē to death or driue thē out of
the realme, as many haue bin thes latter yeares,
vvhat profitt also is ther like to come of this?
let vs gesse of the tyme to come by that which is
past:those hūdreths that haue bine put to death,
haue they done the state good or hurte? abroad
we see thē published for martyres, in al bookes,
tables, pictures and storyes that are vvritten,and
no one thinge euer moued strangers so much to
admire,Inglād as the sight & knowledge of this.

At home their estimation and parties do increase hereby, seing ther is none that eyther is
banished or put to death for this cause, but is
eyther estemed as a martyr or cōfessor, by them,
and so

*Incorue-
niences
by put-
ting so
many mē
to death
for reli-
gion.*

& so eyther in respect of his holynes or in hope he may returne agayne to do them good one day, or for desire of reuenge for his hard vsage, ther is no father, brother, sonne, nephew, kinsman, frende or acquaintance of his left in England which by this is not made a mortal enimye to his persecutors, and how far this may reatch and extend it selfe in such an Iland as Ingland is, or what effects it may worke in tyme to come; I leaue it (sayeth this man) to your wiser considerations.

The increase of seminaries.

Moreouer (sayeth he) I would haue you to consider that before order vvas giuen in Inglish vniuersities at home, to examine schollers and presse them to othes, the Inglish scholler vvas searse hard of in forrayne scholes and vniuersytyes, neyther vvas there mention of Inglish seminaryes to be erected in straynge countries, but after that vppon molestation at home, schollers began to repayre ouer to Doway, and then vppon the practise from Ingland to driue them from thence, they fledd to Rhemes and increased greatly in number (though al left not Doway but for one remayned tvvo places of recourse) and then agayne vppon dealing with the king of france for their expulsion from Rhemes an other Seminary also was erected by the pope in Rome, and after that agayne when this vvas pursued from Ingland by many edictes, an other vvas erected in Valliodolid in Spayne, and after an other proclamation set out agaynst that, an other Seminary presently vvas set vp in Seuil, as
before

before in the narration hath bin touched, and
out of thes haue and do come euery yeare into
Ingland Priestes in such abundance, as my Lord
Treſorer himſelfe confeſſeth that for one that
came into Ingland before, ther commeth now
feuen, and perhapps he might haue ſaid ſeuen-
teene, and albeit aboue a hundreth of them
haue bine put to death, yet more hundreths
grow of them euery day, and in the meane ſpace
her Maieſty waxeth old, the realme groweth to
more diſſention and confuſion in religion, the
Puritans become very hoat and heady, the people
wearyed and amazed, whith thes manner of
procedings, what the ſhalbe thee end at léght of
this courſe think you?

Truely quoth one of the company for this
poynt of the Catholiques, I know not what to
ſaye, the euent being doubtful, for the cauſes &
experience which you haue now alleaged: but
for the puritans I haue hard ſome men of diſcourſe auouch in Ingland, that they will cer-
tainly be extinguiſhed, if the Queenes Maieſtie
liue any number of yeates for that the whol
councell ſemeth fully bent therunto, & were it
not for my L. Treaſorer who is thought to fauour them in ſecret, men iudge that it would
very quickly be brought to paſſe.

Tuſh, you are deceaued ſaid the other, nay
much more poſſible & likely it is that the puritan ſhal ouercome the proteſtant then the contrary: for that the puritan buyldeth directly vppon the proteſtants firſt groundes in religion, &

Whe-ther the Puritans may be rooted ont or not in In-gland.

deduceth

deduceth therof cleárly and by ordinary consequence al his conclusions, which the proteftant
cannot deny by divinity, but only by polhay &
humane ordination, or by turning to catholique
antwers contrary to ther owne principles: and
therfore it is hard for any man finceily to be a
proteftant, but that he wil eafily paffe on alfo
more or leffe to be a puritan: and only they in
effect wilbe agaynft them, who are interelled in
the other fide, as Archb. fhopes, Bilhopes, Atch-
deacons, chanons, notary s, regifters, ciuil la-
wers & the like, for not leefing their cómodityes,
and fome few councellors alfo perhaps for not
offending the Queene, who aboue al others is
intereffed in this aff yre, and yet al thefe, being
but the lefler number in refpect of the multitude (though of moft power for there prefent authority) it fhalbe impoffible to extinguifh the
Puritans, except they extinguifh firft the principles and foundations of proteftants religion, vppon which puritans do grounde.

Which thing my L. Burlev t warrant you
wel vnderftandeth (faveth he) and for that caufe feeketh now to hould fo great a hand with
them, whom he contemned for fome yeares paft,
when they were weaker. And albeit in this
laft parliament to content the Queene, my L. of
Canterbury, and fome others of the councel
that fauour them not, and to get others to ftick
the leffe at yelding to the ftatute agaynft catholiques, he was content alfo to let paffe an acte
agaynft the puritans: yet is it fo qualified with
favorable

fauorable clauses in their behalfe (put in diuers
of them by his honor as is thought after the
parliament ended)as is easily discouered that he
wisheth them vvel, and the very last clause of al
the act, wherin it is sayd, that the vvhole act
shal indure no longer then vntil the next session
of parliament, playnely declareth the great feare
which the vvhole state hath of them, and that
the councel vvalketh on thornes and standeth
doubtful as yet vvhat the euent vvilbe, & how
this first act agaynst the puritanes vvilbe taken
and digested by them, and according to this, assure your selfe the execution of the statute s hal-
be, and consequently feare you not, the extin-
ction of the puritans, but rather lett the protestants loke vvel to themselues vvho haue by
this proceding of my L. Tresorer brought both
puritans and catholiques on their backes. And
vvittely spake Sargeant Owin of late in my Sargeant
Ovvins
opinion, at the Barr agaynst Barrow and Gre- speech of
newode, that vvere araygned and executed, that late,
puritanes and papists vvere like dangerous pio-
ners, that began to digg at the two endes, and
would inclose at the length the protestant in
the middle, and meete at the very hart of the
realme, vnderminyng the same before it could
be remedied: vvhich no doubt by al humane
reason of state and common wealth, must be so,
and cannot long hould out in this course, that
now it followeth, and consequently they vvere
no great vvise men that began the same.

To this discourse al held their peace for a
E   vvhile

vvhile, looking the one vppon the other who
fhould anfwere, vntil at length one fayde. As
The pro-
bilities
that puri-
tanes vill
preuaile.
for the puritans (Sir quoth he) I am fully of your
opinion, that it wilbe a hard peece of vvork to
roote them out, but rather that they are like to
ouercome in the end, both proteftants and papi-
ftes: the proteftants, for the reafons you now
haue giuen, that they do buyld vppon the very
firft groundes of al Inglifh proteftants, that follow Caluins doctrine, and do feme to pretend
but only the perfection and true vfe therof, and
confequently that reafon of yours hath much
fitted my vnderftanding, that their can fcarce be
a zelous Inglifh proteftant (for I meddle not
vvith Lutherans in Germany) but that he vvil
paffe eafily to be a puritan, if fome particuler intereft do not hinder him, which cannot be prefumed of the maior part, and fo in tyme if this
religion hold in Ingland, it muft needes be, that
this partye alfo of the Puritan vvil certaynly
forward in like manner, and preuaile agaynft
the other, but efpecially if once a Prince fhould
enter that did fauour them indede, as eafely
may be imagined, that any other proteftat Prince lightely vvil do, after her Maiefty, vvho fhal
not be fo fetled in this manner of gouerment as
her Maiefty is, nor fo perfwaded agaynft thes
men as this Queene is, and hath bin hitherto
by al her councellors, and by none more perhapps in tyme paft, then by my L. Treforer who
now being of an other mynde and defignement
(as is prefumed) though he dare not vtter it per-
chance

chance to this Queene, yet vvil he eafely finde
reafons to perfwade the fame to an other Prince, that fhal come after, if he liue to that day as
perhapps he may hope to doe, alleaging and
laying before him that now tymes caufes and
circumftances are altered, and feing the puritans
now fo ftrong it may be dangerous to refift
them, and that their religion is not to take any
thing from the Prince, but rather to bring vnto
him; for as the proteftants religion brought
abbyes, Nunryes, and other religious houfes to
the temporal Prince, fo this wil bring Arch-
bifhop rikes, Bifhoprickes, Deanryes, Arch-
deaconryes with other femblable good mor-
fels of welth, by which reafons it vvil not be
hard, to perfwade any other Prince, that hath
not the auerfion imprinted in him as this
Queene hath, to enkendle his zeal to be a puritan. And this is the likelyhoode that I conceaue that puritans wil preuaile in tyme againft
the proteftants: and this tyme I beleeue is not
fo far of as that you fhal euer fee this act now
made agaynft them continued, or renued, in
any other parliament & fo it is likely that thofe
of their partye wel vnderftoode it vvhen they
lett this ftatute paffe in this parliament, rather
to awaken the puritans therby in deed then to
feeke their redreffe or conformitye in religion.
For what? doe you thinke that any Puritan in
the world wil euer be forced to make that forme of recantation and humiliation to the proteftant, which is fet dow_ne in the ftatute? to

Reafons for the puritan religion.

As landes alfo of colleges in tyme.

E 2   vvit,

wit, *that I do humbly confesse and acknowledge that I haue greuously offended god in vsing and frequenting disordered and vnlawfull conuenticles vnder pretence & colour of exercise of religion, &c.* Nay I thinke ve-ryly the protestant (hal first make him eate his communion booke which he so much dete-steth) before he shall driue him to make this recantation. It may chance driue him to buckle with the protestant *de summa rei,* somewhat soo-ner then he had thought before, therby to try which of them shall haue the vpper hand to force the other to recāt, but him I thinke, verely they shal neuer bring vnder, but rather by eg-ging of him put him sooner vp, who first or last wil rise aboue the other, at leastvvise this is my iudgment of the matter take it as you wil.

And as for the papist, me thinke the difficul-ty of victory is much lesse agaynst him, eyther for puritan or protestāt that wilbe ridd of him, seing that now by this act of parliament (as hath bin sayde) they haue him by the legg and so tyed vp & limited, as they may eyther ruine or weary him at their pleasure, whensoeuer oc-casion or need shal require.

An other opinion that puri-tans shal not so easily pre-uaile. To this an other replyed, that as the puritans had great opportunity to grow and go forvvard vvhile the Queene and councel were occupied in repressing papistes, so did not he thinke not-withstanding that their victory vvas so suer or easie on eyther side, that is to say, eyther agaynst protestants or papistes, as this man made it, for

as for

as for the state present (sayeth he) it is certayne
that authoritie is so bent agaynst them, for seing
the ruyne that by them is iminent, as it is like,
they vvil neuer cease to pursue them : & wheras
you say, that ther is neuer a protestant of zeale
but vvil easely passe on to be a puritan , except
he be stayed by interest, it may be so in many,
vvho do only runne forwards from poynt to
poynte of new doctrines and religions , with
such heate and greedines, as they neuer looke
further but to that which is before them, but in
many others it may breed perhapps a contrary
effect, to witt that they vvil rather draw back-
vvards agayne, considering ther is no stay , nor
ende , nor certanty in running so much for-
warde, as we haue seene in our dayes , from papists to Lutherans , from Lutherans to Svvin-
glians , from Swinglians 'to Caluinists , from
Caluinists to puritans , and now last of al from
puritans agayne of a mylder sort , vnto heddy
Brownists , & this effect it is thought this consideration may vvorke, especially in diuers of
the priuy councel it self, who being men of wis-
dom and ryper discourse wil soner fal iuto such
an accompt.

And this for the state present of Ingland: but
as for any other Prince protestant that may suc-
ceade hereafter, the matter is vncertayne how
he vvould be inclined in such a case , and the
reason which you alleaged, that the puritan religion wil take nothing from him , but add
much vnto him, as bishoprickes deanryes and

Of the Prince that shal follovv.

E 3   the like,

the like, it is very doubtful, with me how it would synck into him, and to his councel. For first it is euidēt, that the puritan religion taketh from the Prince al his primacy and authority ecclesiastical, which in a protestant gouerment is one of the chiefest pillars and foundations of al the rest. The Brownists also do take away his authority to make lawes, appoynt orders, & subiecteth him to the excommunications and censures of vulgar ministeres and mutinous cōgregations, and the practise therof we se partly in Scotland where the king is tossed and tumbled by troblesome people as it pleaseth the ministers vvithout heades, to blow into their eares, so as neyther he nor they haue any certainty of stay at all.

The reason also of adding bishoprickes and other ecclesiastical liuings to the crowne is very doubtful and ambiguous with me, for seing they are alredy at the Princes disposition, I see not vvhat great gift or additiō it can be to him, if any man wil pul them downe to his handes: nay it is now by experience of some yeares brought in question, vvhether it vvere profitable euē for temporal respects vnto king Henry the eight, to pul downe the monasteryes altogether and distribute there possessiōs to particular men as he did, or to haue permitted them to stand, and now and then to haue fleezed them of ther wealth, seing many are of opinion (and so am I also) that it is more gaynful to sheer euery yeare a sheepe & now and then to pul of
frute

frute from a tree, then to take at one tyme the woll and flefh of the one, or the frute & vvood together of the other, and this for the protestant.

In like manner I do not think the puritans victory agaynst the papift is like to be fo eafy as you imagin, for as for the maffacre (if any fuch thing fhould be intended as I vvould thinke rather no) at leaft it is not probable that it vvilbe fuffred in this Queenes dayes; firft for the troble and peril that fuch an act might bring vnto the common vvealth: and fecondly for that therby the puritan fhould be ftrengthned and much armed to oppreffe alfo the proteftant, if once this coüterpoyze of the papift vvere cut of. *The Catholiques not fo eafie to be extinguifhed.*

And as for after her Maiefties death, vntil another Prince be fetled, of the many that are like to pretende it may be thought, that the Catholique vvil prouide fufficiently for himfelfe, not to be oppreffed by any fudden violence, which the more eafily he fhalbe able to do, for that it is impoffible any fuch matter to be executed generally without fome former defigmëts conferences and confultations, feing that many muft be the executioners therof, and as impoffible it is, to haue any fuch confultations or defigments, but that fome, notice vvil come to the catholiques before hande, feing ther is no court councel, campe, or company lightly in Ingland, but that it hath fome or other, eyther by confcience, religion, kindred, allyance, frenfhip, obligation or affection deuoted to fome of

E 4   them,

them, yea the very partyes themselues that must be executioners of this act in euery shire, if it be done, let them be as forward other vvise in any religion as they vvil, yet is it impossible but for some of the afore sayd causes they wil shew some frenship, as it is eately sene in al the searches that commonly are commaunded, vvhich being concluded neuer so secretly, are yet commonly fore knowne more or lesse by the Catholiques, and much more wilbe so bloody & boysterous an actió as a massacre or general slaughter vvould be : and therfore my opinon is, that thes three partyes and factions of protestants, puritans, and papistes, vvil buckle together longer yet, then you do imagin, and which part shal haue the vpper hand in the ende, God only knoweth : and therfore if my L. Burley or Sir Nicholas Bacon, might haue auoyded this garboyle in the begining (as some here haue affirmed and it seemeth euident) or might haue tempered the same sithence, vvith a more mylde manner of proceeding vvithout bringing the matter into this disperate contention, or the state into so euident dainger : no doubt but (as you say) they nether vvere nor are to be accoumpted men of grear vvisdome, or gouerment : as some haue esteemed them, thus much vvas spoken of thes assayres.

The conclusion.

Other poynts touching the Lord Burly.

Sundry other poyntes of gouerment came in question at this tyme, and vvere disputed to and fro, and my L. Tresorers prudence therin discussed, as namely and among other thinges his pro-his proceding vvith the nobilitye, vvhether it were true pollicy or no to procede fo vvith the nobility as he hath done, pulling dovvne the principal and holding the reft out of gouermēt, and doings, vvhich was the fal and ruyne of Crumwell, as alfo the holding fo many chiefe offices together in his owne handes, vvhich muft needes be a moft odious poynte, from which in pollicy an ambitious man hath to fly for better eftablifhing of that vvhich he getteth, but in thes things ther were fo many reafons alleaged on the one fide & the other, as it was hard to giue iudgment vvhich vvas to be preferred *in Filijs huius Sæculi.*

Other poyntes ther femed of more impor- Other cō-
tance and confequence as the open breaking fider ations.
with al the old leagues of Ingland, the fpending of fo infinite treafure in forrayne and vnnecef-fary warres, for which any Prince that fhal follow muft needes by al probabilyty cal him or his vnto accompt. The authorifing of fo open and ordinary piracy by vvhich the honor, fubftance, and fubiects of the realme are fo notorioufly damaged, the multitude of ftraingers dravvne into the realme vvhich deuour and im-pouerifh the natural inhabitants : the many bookes pamphletts and proclamations which he hath put forth vvith out confideration, which haue giuen aduantage vnto the enemye : al thes thinges (I fay) though diuers reafons and confi-derations were alleaged to defend or excufe them,

E 5   them,

them: yet inclined the maior part of this conference, to note them rather of some vvant of
iudgment then othewise.

The
Queenes
not mar-
tying.
But of al other thinges the matter of successió
and her Maiestyes not marrying, vvas thonght
by al mens verdicts to make demonstration of
grear and notable vvants in Sir William Cecil
and M. Nicholas Bacon at the begynninge, not
only of mature fore sight and wisdome, but also
of true loue and respect towards their countrey
and fidelity tovvards her Maiesty, for that seing
their only ende in this great affayre to perswade
her Maiesty not to marry, vnder pretence of more fiedome and liberty, and lesse subiectió to her
person, could be no other in truth, but only for
their owne greater power and hand ouer her,
(vvhich they vvel saw could not hold so absolute if she had euer taken a husband) this consideratió ought not to haue preuayled so much
with them, eyther in conscience, reason, or pollicy, but that they should haue looked to the
euent which now draweth on, to wit the peril
of vniuersal distruction to their countrey, wherin them selues, their children, and posterity (for
whose aduauncement they committed this error) are also conteyned.

The L.
Burlyes
gaine by
the Quee-
nes not
marrying.
Truth it is (sayd one of the company) that
they two men and especially my L. Burley, hath
had as long and large and vniforme a reigne
vnder this Queene as euer lightly councellor or
courtyer or fauorite had vnder any prince, and
perhapps

perhapps the like is scarse to be read of, especially so vniforme (as I haue said) that is, so
constant and like it selfe, and stil vvith increase
without ebbes and flowes, rysings and fallyngs
as other wise is accustomed to happen: and certayne it is that the chiefest grownde of al this,
hath bin the Queenes being a sole woman,
who therby hath bin enforced to giue her selfe
wholy into his handes, and any husband that
she might haue had must needes haue abridged
much of this absolute sway, by taking into his
owne handes or to his frendes, some part of the
gouerment, which this man now hath possessed wholy, hauing bin to the Queene both husband, and master, counceller, and gouernour
thes many yeares. But yet seing that the con-
tinuation and confirmation of thes things, and
namely the conseruation of titles, honors, and
riches by thes meanes gotten to his posterity,
dependeth vvholy of the succession of the
crowne (seing her Maiesty cannot liue euer) it
cänot be thought wisdome in my L. Burley that
for the respect of his present particuler sway,
he should suffer the publique (and ther vvith
also his owne for the tyme to come) to fal into
such desperat termes of open peril as now we
see them in, by occasion of her Maiesties not
marrying.

To this one of the conference sayde that he
could not imagin that this matter of succession
remayned so doubtful and dangerous in the

A bout
the suc-
cession.

iudgment

iudgment of my L. Treforer, as it seemed to vs & other men abroade, but that he had some secret and sure designement and plot contriued in his owne head, to put in execution so sone as God shal take her Maiesty frō vs, as the Dukes of Northumberland and Suffolk had in tyme of King Edward the sixte, though other men knew not therof, and especially when they saw the King, not like to liue long, and so when all men looked for a Mary Queene, they came forth with a Queene Iane, and so may this man sayeth he with some Arbella Queene or the like, when least it is expected.

No doubt (sayed a nother) if his designmēt may take place, the lott shal fal vppon some woman or childe, whom he may gouerne as he hath done hitherto, for vnder any male Prince of age, he wil neuer willingly liue, seing hicher to he hath bin master of wardes, both to the realme, Queene, and councel for so many yeares together, and for that ther be so many pretenders now to the crowne as men do saye (for the fame goeth there wanteth not three or fowre at the least) his Lord ship shal not want store to make his choise of.

And that is our misery said a Gētleman law-yer newly come forth of Ingland, that ther be so many pretenders to this garland, which only one can weare: and wheras you say that ther be three or fower, I can auoutch vnto you that ther be more then three tymes three which by

interest

interest of succession may pretend therunto &
stand in hope to get the same.

You meane (said an other) by order of succession in longe tyme to come; nay sayeth he,
I meane immediatly next after the Queene that
now is, and in the first degree. For albeit ther
be among them (as of necessity ther must) diuers and different degrees of discent; yet euery
one of them hath particuler reasons to perswade himselfe and others, that he ought to be
next in possession, and iustly may stand not only
in hope, but also in defence therof by the sword
if he be able, or otherwise by negotiatiõ of his
frendes, and the more part of them are in such
case, as they must neades take armes for tryal
of their title, though they vvould forgo it, for
that no security of peace can be made by them
with their fellow competitors, but vvith armes
in their handes, and then imagin you (quoth
he) when so many of the blood royall shall arme themselues, what shal become of Ingland
and Inglish men.

To this speach of the Gentleman, al that
were present stoode very attentiue, marueling
much to heare him name so great a number of
competitors to the crowne, affirming that they
had neuer hard that ther weare so many, or so
resolute euery man to make good and set for-
warde his particuler title. Some said that in Ingland they had hard in tymes past, that the
Queene of Scots had a title, which men vnderstood

stood commonly, was cut of by her late attainder: some talke also there had bin of the Earle of hertfords children, and now lately of one Arbella whom men saye that the Earle of Licester vvent about to haue marryed her to his sonne, and so to haue made her Queene, some speech ther hath bin also of an old title of the Earle of Huntington, which commonly men thought was litle to the purpose: but of so great a number as this man speaketh of, and that euery parte should hould so pregnant hope of preuayling, they saide they neuer imagined: and desired the Gentleman very earnestly to imparte with them more in patticuler what he knew in that affaire, and so did especially a certayne Ciuilian Lawyer newly come from Italy Spayne and France, wher he had both trauayled and studyed as also he had donne in some partes of Germany, and semed much giuen to matter of state, and therfore made instance to the Gentleman to say some what of this argument, and subiect, offering also to adioyne his verdicte vvhere any thing should offer it selfe within the compasse of his profession reading or experience.

To vvhich the Gentelman answered, this is a matter (quoth) he that I haue studied diuers yeares and conferred in Ingland with men of diuers factions and affections in this behalfe, who though the statute forbid treating of thes poynts, yet in secret do they discourse very largely

gely therof with men whom they dare truſt, and notable packing and negotiation ther is vnder hand about this buſines in ſecret, euery parte for his prince pretended, and nyne or ten plotts I haue hard of, for ſo many perſons that do or may pretend it, all which for that you requeſt me ſayeth he, and do promiſe to ſay your oppinions alſo as occaſion ſhalbe offered, and we are now fallen into that matter, & the the tyme ſerueth conuenient enough, I ſhall here very willingly impart vvith you by vvay of diſcourſe, not fearing the ſtatute of treaſon for determinyng any mans right in ſucceſſion to the crowne, both for that this place is out of Ingland, as alſo for that I meane to determyne nothing at all, but rather to follow the Academical Philoſophers in this affayre whoſe profeſſion was to argue and diſpute on euery ſide, and to conclude nothing: nay my very purpoſe ſhalbe (ſaid he) to ſhew you that I do not know what to conclude, and that the matter is ſo doubtful ambiguous, and diſputable, on euery ſide, as God only and the ſword muſt make the concluſion, and this in my opinion, is the cheifeſt and moſt certayne and very vvorſt poynt of al other in this great buſines.

If this be ſo, (ſaid one of the company) why is ther not order taken by parliament for ſo great an inconuenience, and how commeth it to paſſe that we heare out of Ingland that ſome were committed to priſon this laſt parliament
for offering

VVhy it is for bidden in Ingland to treate of the succession. for offering to treate in this affayre? No marvaile said the Gētleman, for that to treat of this matter now, when ther is none to succed that may be presumed by the neernes of bloode to desire more the Queenes safty then ther owne commodity, (as it would be if she had children of her owne) weare to put her Maiesties state & person in no smale danger, vvhich she prudently foreseing hath for bidden to haue the question debated in her dayes. Wherin no doubt (sayeth he) she hath great reason in al lawe of pollicy: for that she hauing no kynred so neer in bloode as obligatiō of nature may assure her Maiesty of ther fidelity, it were a perilous poynt to make determination of her succession now, for it were to put vp aulter agaynst aulter, and a rising sonne agaynst a falling sonne: It were to fill mens heades with new discourses hopes and designmēts, to moue passions feares enuies hatreds lelozies & ambicions, it were to breed new practises negotiations and canuasses, and to fill the realme with vnquiet humors. And for her Maiesty, it were to gyue her matter of perpetual care, sollicitude and danger for it were in deade to treat of her burial whiles she is yet in health, and to deuide her patrimony whiles she is yet in possessiō, vvhervnto I maruayle not yf she be vnwilling to yeeld.

To this may be added also for iustifying of her Maiesties proceeding in this poynt, so highly mislyked by dyuers sortes of men, that it is not

It is not probable that this prouisiõ if it fhould be made by parliament, for the next fucceffor, and at this tyme, and as things now ftande, would be greatly auaylable eyther to the realme, or to the party in whofe fauour it fhould be made, not to the realme, for that vvee fee by many experiences of actes of parliaments made for fucceffion both in King Henry the eight his tyme, and much more before, in tyme of controuerfy betwene the two houfes of Lancafter and York, as alfo before that agayne in King Richard the firft his dayes, for the fuccef-fion of Artur the Duke of Britany, and other the like, actes, that they were neuer obferued or refpected afterwards, when a ftronger pretendor came to plead his caufe, fo as thofe actes ferued for nothing els but to exafperate more the competitor agaynft vvhom they vvere made.

To the partye alfo for whom they fhould be made, they do fealdom any good at al, but rather do put him in far greater dainger then before; and namely they would do fo now in Ingland, things ftanding ther as they do, to witt, the Prince in poffeffion being fo far of in kyndred as fhe muft needes liue in Ielofy of that party, and the other competitors being fo many, ftrong and apparent in ther pretences, as they may be egged heerby to work the diftruction both of the one & the other: for al which refpects and many other that may be alleaged,

F   thinke

I thinke this order taken in Ingland, not only needful, but reasonable also and commodious, said this Gentleman.

No doubt said the Ciuilian, but it is commodious yf you respect the present only, for that it doth eschu both garboyles to the realme and cares and periles to both partyes as you haue said, I meane both to the Queene and her heyre apparent that should be declared, who must needes be a mortal enimye vnto her Maiesty the very first hower that he is declared, for that his next desire after such declaration once obteyned must needs be, that her Maiesty were quickly dead, and he or she in her place; and for that her Maiesty must needs know and feare this, & the other must needs imagine, that she knowing and fearing it, would seeke to preuent the same, betwene thes feares I say and hopes, thes hatreds and suspitions, thes ambitions and Ielosyes, no peace frenship or long endurance could be expected. And for that the hopes and hartes of men, are set commonly much more vppon the Prince that is to come or rising, then vppō him that is in fading, the greater dainger were like to fall vppon the present possessor, wherof I could gyue (you said he) if neede weere, diuers examples out of storyes of our profession, I meane pertayning to the study of our emperial lawes, by which is made most euident, that more Cæsars (vvho vvere heyres apparent to the empire as you know) haue put

Note this poynt.

haue put downe Emperors, then Emperors haue byn able to restrayne *Cæsars* albeit them selues were able to make them, so as to the Prince
in present possession it is (no doubt) very secure
and commodious to haue this prohibition, and
that the right of succession do hange obscure
and doubtfull, and no lesse profitable is it also in
my opinion to al the competitors, for that by
this meanes they haue tyme euery man to prepare his frendes & worke his cause vnderhand,
wheras if any should be declared the rest
should be iniured & therby also exasperated &
him selfe putt in place of enuy and dainger
without power of defence, as hath byn said, but
after her Maiestyes death, if he put vp him selfe,
it is like he wil haue a party to stick by him to
enable his demaund.

And this is for the present during her Maiesties life: but as for the future tyme it must needes be a terrible threatening of extreme calami-
tye to the common wealth to haue so many lye
in wait to assayle her, as you haue signified do
pretend the crowne , which truly I confesse
(sayeth he) with the residew here (though
somevvhat perhaps I haue studyed and read
more then euery one of this company) that I
neuer estemed to be so many in number, and
much lesse of such consideration for their titles,
as you seeme to hold them, and therfore I pray
you defer no longer to begynne the discourse
vvhich you haue promised and we al desyre.

The

The Gentleman answered that he was content, and so began presently, and for more perspecuitye sake he reduced al the present pretenders to the crowne after the Queene that now is, to three principal heades or branches, to witt to the house of lancaster a part, to the house of Yorck a part, and to the last coniunction of both houses in Kyng Henry the seuenth, assigning three competitors of the first branch, and three of the second, and fower of the last, of al whose titles he discoursed largely at diueres metings for three or fower dayes one after another, and the Ciuilian also said his parte, & some others put in their verdicts as occasion vvas offred, but the two former spake most and shewed great reading, and had not the Gentleman shewed himselfe somewhat to partial some tymes agaynst the Catholique in matters of religion as one that had byn brought vp only in Ingland he had fitted greatly my humor, but yours he vvould haue fitted the more for this, but in truth his speach in this matter of the succession was very pithy, and founded in great reason and authority without partiality to any party, and I assure my selfe that you would haue liked it extremly well if you had hard it, and I presuppose that some of the company hath taken it in paper though I know not vveil as yet, nor haue I now any tyme to enquire the truth, for that the post is vppon his departure, and I will not keepe this letter by me any longer and

A diuisiõ of the pretéders to the crovene.

ger and now it groweth to fome bigger bulck
alfo then at the beginyng I had intended it,
wherfore I fhall here make an ende, and if I
can gett the other difcourfe hereafter concerning the fucceffion you may perhapps haue A dif-
a fight therof alfo, for I know it wil yeld you the fuc-
very great contentment. God keepe you, ceffion
promifed.
at *Amfterdam* in Holland this firft
of September 1593.

F I N.

RICHARD SMITH

A Brief Inquisition

1630

A BRIEF INQVISITION

INTO

F. NICHOLAS SMITH

his Discussion of

M. D. KELLISON

his Treatise of the Ecclesiasticall Hierarchie.

Deuided into XII. *Sections.*

By a Deuine.

AT DOWAY,

By the widdowe of MARKE WYON
at the signe of the Phenix.

M. DC. XXX.

Priuatæ causæ pietatis aguntur obtentu, & cupiditatum quisque suarum Religionem habet velut pedissequam. *Leo. Epist.* 52. *ad Theodos. Imper.*

APPROBATIO.

VIso testimonio cuiusdam mihi probè noti, censui hunc libellum, cui titulus: *Brenis Inquisitio in* Nicolai Smithæi *discussionem tractatus* Domini Kellison *de Ecclesiastica Hierarchia* vtiliter imprimi posse, vtpote nihil continentem fidei aut bonis moribus aduersum. Actum Duaci Kalend. Iunij 1630.

GEORGIVS COLVENERIVS *S. Theol. Regius ordinariúsque Professor, Collegiatæ Ecclesiæ S. Petri Præpositus & Canonicus, Duacensis Academiæ Cancellarius, ac librorum Censor.*

Preface to the Reader.

THere haue been of late sett forth in English diuers bookes, by some English Protestants, against the Catholike faith, wherein some Iesuits and Mōkes haue been impugned and challenged by name; which bookes haue doon much hurt in Religion, and it hath been greatlie wished, that either the sayd Religious persons, or some of theyr order had answered those bookes, which hithertoe none of them haue doone.

But whiles in the meane tyme M. Doctor Kellison putteth forth a booke nether against, nor for anie man, but onelie in defence of the Ecclesiasticall Hierarchie of Gods Church, albeit it was written so soundlie and so moderatelie as one of the auncientest and learnedest of the Benedictins in England sayd, he could find no fault with the

the doctrin: yet because it see-
ved by setting forth Episco-
pall dignitie, to obscure and
shaddowe Regular profession;
streight wayes a Iesuit could
find both leasure and meanes
in England to print a Pam-
phlet which he termeth A
modest Discussió of some
points taught by M. Do-
ctor Kellison &c. *wherein*
by vaine cauills and Sophis-
mes, which anie student in
Logick might as well alledge
against the orthodoxall wri-
tings of anie auncient Father
or other classicall Author, he

A 3 *takes*

takes vpõ him to ouerthrowe some of the chiefe grounds and arguments of M. D. Kellisons *booke, and soe to purchase vnto himselfe with the vnlearned and vulgar sorte, the name of a doughtie writer (forsooth) in diuinitie.*

But *the iudicious and vn-partiall* Reader *of both theyr writings, will smile to him selfe, and say* Impar congressus; *and will soone discouer the* Discussors *weakenesse and temeritie, whose chiefe drift indeed was to disgrace the* Doctor, *to de-presse*

presse Episcopall authoritie, to extenuate the vertue and necessitie of one of Gods Sacraments, and insteed of all this, to exalt and magnifie a Regular State of life, such as himselfe professeth. Egregiam vero laudem!

VVhy these men, that professe learning and Religion, should bee slow to answere bookes written both against them selues, and the Catholike faith, & soe quick and readie to write against those bookes which were written nether against them,

nor

nor the Catholike faith, but rather for a high point of the Catholike faith, I leaue to others to difcuffe.

And albeit I doubt not but that fome of M. D. Kellifons fchollers will replie to this Pamphlet more at large, and defend his doctrine, which in all points will be found to bee found and fubftantiall, yet becaufe fome of theyr followers (as I heare) doe much magnifie the fame, euen before they haue reade it : I haue, at the requeft of a freind, made this briefe Inquifition into it: wherein

wherein I haue not exactly noted whatsoeuer is worthy of Cenſure, but onely what occurred vnto me ſuddainly.

The Authour, as I am told for certaine, is a Ieſuit, whoſe ſurname beginneth whith the ſame letter that D. Kel-liſons *ſurname doth, vnder whome, I vnderſtand hee hath been breddeheretefore in* Doway Colledge *, though now he ſeeketh to bee aboue him and to crow ouer him, contrary to that ſayng of our bleſſed Sauiour*[*] non eſt diſ-cipulus ſuper magiſtrum ſuum.

Mat
cap.
v. 2.

A 5

suum . *VVherefore I will, for breuities sake, vnderstand* Doct. Kellisons *name by* D. K. *and the Discussors by* F. K. *and soe lett vs proceede to the* Inquisition *and see what wee find worthy of* Censure *in him.*

ABOVT

ABOVT
THE AVTHOVR
AND PVBLISHER
OF THE DISCVSSION.

SECTION I.

HE Author of this Dif-
cuffion is faied to be
Nicolas Smith, who
was a Iefuite, and died
fome months agoe; but in the *Ad-*
uertiffement to the Reader, he is
faied to haue difliked the publishing thereof. The Publisher is pretended to be a lay man, and he
namelesse. It cometh forth, with-

A 6   out

2

out either the Approbation of any,
or the Permiſſion of ſuperiours, as
theſe mens books in England cōmonly vſe to doe: which is a tacite
condemnation, both of the booke,
and of the publication of it. For, if
either of theſe be found fault withall by lawfull authority, there is
none extant to iuſtify them, or to
be reprehended for them; And if
they be not diſliked, there will not
wante thoſe, who will auouch
them. Whence I pray you cometh
this fearefull kind of proceeding,
but of their owne diſtruſt both of
the booke, and the publishing of it?

an.
20 *Qui malè agit odit lucem, & non ve-
nit ad lucem vt non arguantur opera
eius.* Contrarywiſe *D. Kelliſon* did
not onely putte his name to his
booke, but alſo procured it to be
approued by publike authority, as
confident of that which he wrotte.

SEC-

SECTION II.

About the Title of the booke.

THE booke is termed *A modest Discussion:* and *q. 5. §. 21.* the Author saieth: *I am resolued not to giue any offence :* and yet is it most full of immodest Sarcasmes, bitter scoffes and gibes, which no way become a modest man to giue, especially to so graue, so venerable, and well deseruing a man as *D. Kellison* is knowne to be. Likewise it is full of vaine ostentations and bragges of his owne proofes and arguments. I will giue some small tast of both. *pag. 16.* he termeth *D. Kellisons* argument *a doughty argument,* which neuerthelesse, (as we shall see hereafter) is the very same,

that

4.

that *Bellarmin* and Catholikes vfe
againft heretiks:and in trueth a de-
monftration *à Negatione definitionis
ad negationē definiti.*Pag.10.Hefaieth
of *D. Kellifon* that he was miftakē
in a thing, which required *No
more learning, then vnderftanding
Latin.* pag.28. *His reafon deferneth no
anfwere.*p.39.*I will not fay noDeuine,
but euen no man in his right iudgment
can affirme.* p.48.*I cãnot but wonder,
that a learned man should vfe fuch a
forme of argumēt.*p.84.*StillM.Doctor
citeth Authors, which proue againft
himfelfe.* p. 89. *Still M.Doctor hath
ill fortune in alleaging Authors.*Thus
he. And diuers other like fpeaches
he hath in this kind.

Of his owne proofs he fpeaketh
thus *qu.1. §.12.p.8.All which principles are by vs demonftrated to haue no
groūd at all.*q.4.§.12.p.77.*I haue demonftrated it not to be probable.* ib. §.
17.p.87.*Confirmation giueth not fuch a
perfe-*

*perfection, as may not be gotten by
other meanes, as we haue demonstrated,
and cannot be denied &c.*

That the Author fauoureth Heretikes againſt Catholikes.

SECTION III.

IN his ſecond queſtion §.2.& ſe-
quent. he denieth, that it can be
proued out of that definition of a
Church giuen by S. Cyprian.epiſt.
69.*Ecclesia eſt plebs Sacerdoti adunata*, that a Biſhop is neceſſary to the
making of a Church: which thing
neuertheleſſe Catholikes do proue
out of it againſt Heretikes, as is to
be ſeene in *Bellarmin lib. 4. de Ecclef. c. 8.*

   *Quæſt.*4.§.16. He denieth S. Clements Epiſtle *to be ſo autheticall, as to*
ſettle

settle thereon a doctrinall point: which
is to fauour Heretiks against Catholiks, who out of those Epistles,
and such others do proue greater
points, then the necessitie of Confirmation. And vpon them are Setled diuers decrees of the Canon
law, as is to be seene in *Gratian.* 16.
q. 1. and in other places. And howfoeuer some Catholiks do doubt of
the Author of these Epistles, yet
Catholiks maintaine their authoritie, as is to be seene by *Turrianus*
in his Treatise *De Epistolis decreta-*
libus : and what scruple *Bellarmin*
findeth, himselfe confesseth, is not
in the copie of the Vatican.*And to
make question of the authority of
S. Clements epistles, is to take part
with heretiks, who reiect their authority. Besides *S. Clement* herein
saieth nothing, but what *S. Vrban,*
S. Cornelius, S. *Cyprian,* S. *Cyrill,*
the Councell of Orleans , the Ca-
nons

Cate-
bif-
uus
d Pa-
ochos.
a.de
Con-
rm.
ro-
teth
ut of
t that
Con-
irma-
ion is
Sa-
ra-
ment,

ṅons of the Church, and vniuer-
fally *the ancient Fathers* do fay.

He fauoureth alfo heretiks in de-
nying *Confirmation* to be neceffarie to Chriſtians , or to be a perfection or complement of their Ba-
ptiſme, and in diuers other pointes,
as we ſhall ſee in the next ſection.

SECTION IV.

He teacheth erroneous doctrine.

QVÆST. 1. §. 8. He taxeth
Doctor Kelliſon for auouching
*all thoſe who haue not had the Sacra-
ment of Confirmation not to be perfect
Chriſtians*, which faieth he, *is vntrue.*
The like he hath often *quæſt.* 4. *per
totam* , which fauoureth of the
doctrine of the heretikes of our
time , as may be gathered out of
Bellarm.

Bellar.l.2. de Sacr.c.28. Where hauing prooued against the *Lutherans*
that Confirmation excelleth all Sacraments for giuing of grace to do
well, he addeth: *Cypriā and Cornelius*
were not afraied to say, they are not fully
sanĉtified, nor perfeĉt Christians, who
want the Sacrament of Chrisme, albeit
Caluin and Kēnitius call this an ancient
Contumelie. Do not S. *Cyprian,* S. *Cor-*
nelius, and *Bellarmin* with them, say
as D. *Kellison* saieth, that who haue
not the Sacrament of *Confirmation,*
are not perfeĉt Christians? And do
not *Caluin and Kemnitius* call this a
contumelie, as F.K. calleth it an
vntrueth? *Henriquez lib. 3. cap. 7.*
Some fathers say, that without Confir-
mation the vertue giuen by baptisme is
not wholie perfeĉt, and that by Confir-
mation one is fullie made a Christian.
And he alledgeth very manie fathers. Againe: *Confirmation is called*
by the fathers the complement of Bap-
tisme.

Ca-
chif.
d pa-
pch.
aieth
bat by
Cōfir-
matiō
ne be-
ometh
e be a
perfeĉt
Soul-
dier of
Christ,
beco-
meth a
man,
recea-
ueth
treigth
of a
perfeĉt
mynde.
hath
the
forme
of a
Chri-
stian.

tifme. Canisius in his Catechisme.
cap. de Confirmatione §. 5. *He
is no perfect Christian who is not confirmed*, thus he deliuering the common doctrine of the Church.

Qu.4.per totam. He denieth the Sacrament of *Confirmatiõ* to be necef-
sary to saluation, which is directly
againft the *Councell of Trent*, the *Pro-
profession of faith* made by Pius IV.
and the doctrine of Catholiks, who
write againft heretiks, and tax
them for it. The Councell Sess.
7. can. 4. saieth *If any say, that the
Sacraments of the new law are not necessarie to saluation, but superfluous, and
that without them, or defire of them,
men may obtaine of God the grace of
iuftification, albeit all of them be not
necessarie to euerie one, be he accurfed.*
Wherein is defined, that *all Sacraments,* (and consequently *Confirmation*) are neceffary to saluation,
as appeareth both by the indefinite
vfe

vſe of the word *Sacraments*, to which the Councell would haue putte the determinat particle *Some*, if it had meant but *of ſome* : and alſo becauſe in the reſtriction, it ſaieth, that *all* Sacraments are not neceſſary to *euerie one* : and likewiſe becauſe *Bellarmin* ſo expoundeth the Councell. But particularly becauſe *Pius quartus* in his profeſſion of faith, where he repeateth theſe words of the Councell, addeth to them *Seauen*, Saying, *Seauen Sacraments are neceſſarie.* Now when the Councell excepteth, that all Sacraments are neceſſarie to *euerie one*, it excepteth not *Confirmation* from this neceſſitie, but onely *Order* and *Matrimonie*, as *Bellarmin* declareth in theſe words libr.1. de Sacrament. cap. 22. *The Councell defineth three things. 1. that Sacraments are neceſſarie. 2. that ſome are ſo ne-*

so necessary, as without them or desire of them saluation cannot be had. 3. *that all Sacraments are not necessarie to euery one, which is saied for Orders and Matrimonie.* And it is euident, for, if *Confirmation* be necessarie to any, it is necessarie * to euery one in the like case, becaufe it is inftituted for the good of euerie particular, and not for the good of the whole Church, as Order and Matrimonie are.

Likewife in our profeffion of faith made by *Pius Quartus* we thus profeffe: *I profeffe also, that there are seauen Sacraments of the new law, inftituted by our Lord Iesu Chrift, and neceffarie to the Saluation of mankind, albeit not all of them to euerie one, to wit, Baptifme, Confirmatiō &c.* where is plainely auouched, that all the 7. Sacraments, (and confequētly confirmation) are neceffarie to the saluation

uation of mankind, though *all* of
them be not so necessarie to *euerie
one.* In like sorte *Bellarmin cap.* 22.
citat. prop. 2. putteth downe this
conclusion: *All Sacraments are necessarie by necessitie of precept, albeit
not to euerie one.* And likewise this
other: *prop.* 4. *The Eucharist, Confirmation and extreme Vnction are necessarie by necessitie of meanes to perfection, or welbeing, Supposing Gods
institution* ; and then saieth of heretiks: *Indeed they acknowledge no necef-
sitie, albeit falselie they say they doe, but
onelie some small vtilitie of Sacramets.*
And lib. 2. *de Sacramen. Confirma-
tionis ca.*2.§.Sed hæc etiam solutio.
*The Apostle to the Hebrews 6. c. doth
reckon imposition of hands* (by Confirmation) *with baptisme, with faith,
with pennance, with other things,
which appertaine to saluation, yea
euen to the foundation of religion,
as there the Apostle saieth.*

Where-

Whereby we fee, that to deny the
neceffitie of *Confirmatiõ* and onelie
to graunt vtilitie of it, is to ioyne
with heretikes. Yea to denie that it
appertaineth to the foundation of
Chriftian Religion, is to gainfay
the Apoftle : and yet what other
faieth F. K. q. 4. §. 17. the like. q.
4. §. 3. We graunt (faieth he) *that*
Confirmation giueth a perfection to the
Receaner, but not fuch a perfection, as
may not be gotten by other meanes, as
we haue demonftrated, and cannot be
denied. But how is *Confirmation* neceffarie *Neceffitate medij ad bene effe*,
fe, that is, by a neceffity of meanes
to perfection or wellbeing, if that
perfection or wellbeing, which it
giueth, cã be had by other meanes?
How can this mã teach any neceffitie of *Confirmation*, but onely
fome vtilitie, as Heretikes teach
of Sacraments ? How hath he
demonftrated, or how cannot
that

that be denied, which *Bellarm,* condemneth in heretiks? How can such a man say that *Confirmation* appertaineth to the foundation of Christian Religion?

Quæst 5. §. 2. he saieth : *The state of a Bishop yeeldeth not means to perfection, but onelie presupposeth that the person by other meanes hath gotten perfection.* Et §. 5. *The Bishop is in a state which presupposeth, but doth not giue perfection.* Now, to say, that the state of a Bishop giueth not perfection, or yeeldeth not meanes to perfection, is erroneous. For this is to deny, that *Ordo Episcopalis,* Episcopall Order is a Sacrament, or giueth grace, for, if it giue grace, it giueth perfection and meanes to continew. But that episcopall Order is a Sacrament and giueth grace Bellarm. l. 1. de Sacram. Ordinis. c.5. prooueth at large out of Scripture, fathers and reason, and calleth

calleth it *certissimam assertionem*, a
most certaine assertion : and as Vi-
̴orellus saieth in Tolet.l.1.cap.50.
Valentia tom.4.d.9. q.1. saieth it is
a point of faith.

Quæst. 6. §. 4. he saieth : *Reli-*
gious Superiours who by their office are
immoueable and perpetuall, whereby
they are properlie in state, and are
obliged to gouerne, illuminat, and per-
fecte others, which are acts of perfe-
ction, are truely in a state of perfection
both to be acquired, and already ac-
quired, and in that respect are in some
particular manner and degree of the
Ecclesiasticall hierarchie, more then se-
cular Bishops euen Ordinaries. Which
is in effecte to say, that such *Regular*
Superiours, are in some manner and
degree, more of the Hierarchie, thẽ
the Pope, who is a Secular Bishop
& Ordinary. And can any (I pray
you) in any degree be more of the
Hierarchie, then the Head of the

the

Hierarchie. Besides, thus saieth the Councell of Trent. Sess. 23. c. 4. *The sacred Councell declareth, that besides other Ecclesiasticall degrees, Bishops, who succeede in the place of the Apostles, especially belong to this hierarchicall Order.* And are any *Regular Superiours* in some degree aboue those in the *Ecclesiasticall Hierarchie*, Who chiefly make the hierarchie, & succeede the Apostles? Were there any, in any degree aboue the Apostles in the hierarchie?

That

Section V.

*That either fondly or equi-
uocally, he saieth that Religious as Religious be of
the Hierarchie.*

Qvæst.6. §. 5. p.170. he saieth
*Religious as Religious be of the
Hierarchie*: and §. 6. p. 172. that *they
are in the Hierarchie in a high degree.*
But this is either fondly or equiuo-
cally spoken. For whereas one may
be twoe wayes of a kingdome, either as Prince or magistrat to commaunde: or as subiects to be commaunded; So one may be of the
Hierarchie either as *Hierarchá qui
præst,* as a Prince to commaúde, or
as other to be commaunded. For as
himselfe citeth out of *S. Thomas* 1.
part. q. 108. *art.* 1. *A Hierarchie is a*
B 2   *holy*

holic Principality, *and by the name of* *Principality twoe things are vnder-* *stood, to wtt, the Prince himselfe and a* *multitude ordered vnder the Prince.* Now saieth F. K. *are not Religious* *men a multitude ordered vnder the* *Pope.* True, but yet as vnder the Prince or Hierarch, not as Hierarches themselues. No man euer doubted, but that *Religious* as *Religious* are of the Hierarchie as sub-iects of the Hierarchs, for, so are all kind of Catholiks euen lay men and women. But the question only is whether *Religious* as *Religious* be of the Hierarchie as Hierarches, as Bishops and Priests be? S. *Denis* *de Hierar. c. 6.* maketh twoe orders in the Ecclesiasticall Hierarchie, and in the one he placeth the Hierar-ches, in the other these that are vn-der them: and in both these orders he putteth three degrees, the lowest order of Hierarches, he maketh of

Dea-

Deacons, who (ſaieth he) do purge; the ſecond of *Prieſts,* who do illuminate; and the higheſt of *Biſhops,* who do conſummate. And of the order of thoſe that are vnder the Hierarches, the loweſt order he maketh of *Publik penitents* who are not admitted to the Sacraments, the middeſt of thoſe who are admitted to the Sacraments, and the higheſt of Monkes. So that though he ſay, that Monkes are the higheſt degree of thoſe that are perfected by the Hierarches, and aboue the reſt of the laity, yet he putteth them not in any degree of Hierarches. Whereupon thus writeth Bellarmin lib. 1. de ordine c. 7. *Deacons can performe almoſt all the offices of Prieſts and Biſhops in their abſence. And this ſeemeth to be the reaſon, why deacons appartaine to the Hièrarchie, and are ſaied to gouerne people, as it appeareth out of ſaint Hicrome in c. 2. ad Tit. and ont of S.*

     Denis,

Denis, who *putteth but these three or-*
ders (of Bishops, Priests, Deacons)
in the Ecclesiasticall Hierarchie, because
these alone are hierarchicall: for the infe-
riour orders do not gouerne the people
but only serue the higher orders. Doe
you heare the reason, why Deacons
appartaine to the Hierarchie, to
witt, because they can do almoſt
all the offices of Bishops & Prieſts?
Do you heare how *S. Denis* putteth
but Bishops, Prieſts, and Deacons,
in the Ecclesiasticall hierarchie? Do
you heare, how these alone are hierarchicall, because they alone do
gouerne the people? And how doth
this agree to religious as religious?
And as for his proofes out of *S. Denis*
and *S. Thomas*, that Religions as
Religious are of the hierarchie,
they are partly corruptions, partly
equiuocall.

Qu. cit. n. 6. he proueth this out
of *S. Denis* de Eccl. hierarch. c. r.

qui.

*Qui hierarchiam dixerit, omnium simul
sacrorum ordinum dixerit dispositionem*
that is, who saieth a Hierarchie, saieth
the disposition of all holy orders together; and then he proueth, that by
Ordinū he meaneth *Institutes or professions,* because before he had saied;
*Hierarchia nostra dicitur esse ratio
complectens sacra omnia quæ ad eam
pertinent.* Our *hierarchie is saied to be
that which comprehendeth all holy
things that belong vnto it.* And c. 6.
cit. *Summus eorum omnium qui ini-
tiantur & perficiuntur ordo est Sancto-
rum Monachorum: The chief order of all
them that are initiated and perfected is
that of holy Monkes.* But here is **S.
Denis** corrupted. For in *S. Denis,*
translated by Ambrose Generall of
the Camaldulan Monkes, is not, *qui
hierarchiam dixerit,* but, *qui sacerdotium dixerit,* and that so it should be,
appeareth by that which followeth:
Ita qui sacerdotem seu Pontificem dicit,

B 4   *augu-*

augustiorem prorsusque diuinum virum insinuat; *So he who saieth a Priest or Bishop, doth insinuat a more sublime and altogether a deuine man.* And immediatly before he saied, that *Sacerdotij nomine honoratus, princeps erit omnium, quæ sacratißima sunt* : *He that is honoured with the name of Priesthood shalbe the Prince of all things, that are most holy.* So that he compareth Priesthood, and Priests together Likewise, he saieth not, as F.K. reporteth, *Sacrorum ordinum* , *of holy orders or institutes:* but he saieth, *Sacrorum simul omnium vno vocabulo signauit ordinem* : *he hath signed in on word the order of all holy things together.* So that *hierarchia, hierarchie* is put for *sacerdotium, priesthood* , and the word *ordinum,* orders (wherof dependeth all his proof) is added to *sacrorum, holy.* And though S. Denis say *Initiandorum omnium sublimior est ordo monachorum.* Of those that

are

are to be initiated, the highest order is that of *Monkes*: yet he saieth not, nor dare F. K. say, that *Ecclesiasticæ Hierarchiæ summus ordo est monachorum*: That the *Monkes* are the chiefe of the *Ecclesiasticall Hierarchie*.

His proof out of *S. Thomas* is equiuocall. For *S. Thomas* indeed sayth that *Hierarchia est sacer principatus*, and that *In nomine Principatus duo intelliguntur, scilicet ipse princeps & multitudo ordinata sub Principe*, but this will not proue that Religious are of the Hierarchie more then the Laitie; for they are *Multitudo ordinata sub Principe*, as subiects are of the kingdome as subiects, but not as Magiftrates or Princes. But when the queftion is whether *Religious* be of the Hierarchie, the fenfe is whether they be not vnder a Prince as subiects, but as Hierarches, or, *Sacri Principes*, as Bishops & Priefts are. And this S. Thomas neither

B 5   faieth

sayth, nor insinuateth. Besides, not only men but women are Religious, and not only those of the Quire, but also lay Brothers and lay Sisters: and who will simply say, that lay Brothers and lay Sisters, are of the Hierarchie, and that also in a high degree? vnles he meane to make the Hierarchie, of the Church ridiculous? Moreouer euen married men, who vse their mariage as lay men doe, may be true Religious men, as the Kinghts of S. Iames, Calatraua, and the like, are. For, thus writeth Nauar a Religious man Consil. 13. de Regul. *Mariage may stand with Religion by dispensation of the Sea Apostolick according to the common opinion of Innocent, of the Glosse, and of others, vpon the chapter, Cum ad monasterium: which Caietan followeth, and we also in our Manuall c. 12. and more largely in comment. 2. de Regul.* And Sanchez a Iesuit *lib.*

4. *de*

4. de decalog. cap. 16. *n.* 11. speaking of the saied knights, saieth, *I think they are true Religious men.* And he citeth many learned men, who, saieth he, mantaine that they are true Religious men; and he addeth *Mota lib. de confir. Relig. c.* 1. *defendeth this point excellently, largely answering to obiections and bringing the subscriptions of most deuines of great name of all Religions:* See also *Suarez tom.* 3. *de Relig. libr.* 9. *c.* 26. *n.* 9. Now, what a sacred Principality, I pray you, is the hierarchie, if not only men, but women, and not only single persons, but euen maried persons be of the Hierarchie? and that in a highe degree? Yea, if they be perpetuall superiours of their Orders, in some degree of the hierarchie, aboue secular Bishops, though ordinaries?

By what hath beene saied of the compatibility of a Religious state with mariage F. K. may temper

what

what he saieth q. 5. n. 8. *for my part I had rather want whatsoever perfe-Ction, wherein a Bishop may surpasse a Religious man, then be in a state not requiring of its nature and essence cha-stitie.* Because it is not true that Religion of it nature and essence requireth chastitie, nay it farre lesse requireth it then the state of a Bishop. For, wee see that the Church dispēseth with diuers orders of kinghts to be true Religious, and yet to marry, euen after their vow of Religion. But it was neuer yet heard of, that the Church permitted a Bishop remaining Bishop to marry, or yet to vse mariage before contracted, and as *Bellarm. l. 1. de clericis c. 19.* saieth against Caluin, *Nullum exemplum in contrarium adferri potest:* No example to the contrarie can be brought. So that chastitie is no more of the essence of Religion, then of Episcopall state, and lesse of Eccle-

cept

ffasticall precept, becaufe this precept was neuer difpenfed withall
in Epifcopall ftate, and it is vfually
difpenfed withall in diuers Religious Orders.

Section VI.

How ignorant he is in ar-
guing: and in Logick, he
argueth ridiculouſly.

QV. 3. §. 12. p. 47. he relateth
this argument of *D. Kelliſons*
for neceſſitie of Bishops in euerie
notable part of the Church: *By diui-*
ne law there muſt be particuler Biſhops
in the Church: but there is no more rea-
ſon why the Church of France, *for*
example, ſhould be gouerned by a Biſhop
then the Church of England, *ergo* England, *and all particuler Churches of*
extent muſt be gouerned by particular
Biſhops . And then ſaieth , *I cannot*
but wonder that a learned man ſhould
                                      make

make such an argument, which he cānot but know, doth faile in a thousand instances. For example, some meat is absolutlie necessarie for the maintenance of man: but there is no more reason why egges or fish should be necessarie rather then other particular meats, ergo egges, fish and all other particular meats are necessarie for the maintenance of man: Or (saieth he) to bring an example neerer to the purpose: It is of the law of God and nature that some mē do marrie for the preseruing of mankinde: But if wee precifelie respect the law of nature, there is no more reason, why one person, village, or cittie is obliged to marrie &c.

But this arguing or comparing of these arguments with that of D. **Kellisons** is ridiculous, and I wonder that a learned man should think them alike. For, D. *Kellison* argueth from the necessitie of some ends to haue such a meanes, to the necessitie.

fitie of euerie end of the like nature to haue the fame meanes. Which kind of arguing is ftrong and good, becaufe euerie end of the like nature,hath like neceffitie. As if meat be neceffarie to fome members of the bodie, then to all; if meat be neceffarie to fome man, then to all; if a captaine to fome armie, then to all; if a Pilot to fome shippe,then to all; If sherrifes be neceffarie to fome shiers, then to all; if Bishops be *de iure diuino* neceffarie for fome particular Churches, then to all Churches of the like nature. And F. K. his argument or comparifon is of the neceffitie of the meane, for example,of the neceffitie of meat to maintaine mākinde:as if *D. Kellifons* argumēt had beene in this fort:Bishops are neceffarie to the Church, *ergo* this, or that Bishop is neceffarie.This argumēt had beene like to that of F,K.For,it had beene from the

the neceſſitie of ſome indeterminat meane to the neceſſitie of ſome determinat meane, as F. K. his argument is. But it is ridiculous to argue from the neceſſitie of one end to haue ſuch a meane, to the neceſſitie of euerie end of the like nature, To the neceſſitie of ſome meanes to the neceſſitie of anie determinat meanes. As if, becauſe we may thus argue (as *D. Kelliſon* doth) Meat is neceſſarie to ſome men, *ergo* to euerie man : Mariage is neceſſarie to the propagation of mankind in ſome country, *ergo* in euery country; one might argue with F. K. ſome meat is neceſſarie to men, *ergo* egges or fiſh : mariage in ſome is neceſſarie for mankind, *ergo* in Peeter. Where we ſee, that the particle *ſome* in that kind of *D. Kelliſons* arguments is ioyned to that word which ſignifieth the *end*, to witt to *Men*, and *Mankind*; whereas in F. K. his arguments

guments the particle *some* is ioyned
to the words that signifie the
Meanes, to wit, to *Meat* and *Mariage*.

In like sort when *D. Kellison*
argued with *Bellarmin l. 4. de Eccles.
c. 8.* and Catholicks commonly,
that there can be no Church without a Bishop, out of that definition
of *S. Cyprian ep. 69. Ecclesia est plebs
sacerdoti adunata, & pastori suo grex
adhærens: A Church is people vnited to
a Bishop, and a flock adhering to there
Pastor*, which argument in trueth is
*à negatione definitionis, ad negationem
definiti:* As such a thing is not a reasonable creature, *Therefore* no man:
Such a nation hath no King, *ergo*
it is no kingdome. For, how can
that Church be vnited to a Bishop,
which hath none, seeing vnion sup-
poseth the being of that to which
one is vnited?

F. K. qu. 2. §. 6. p. 16. termeth
this *a doughty argument* and saieth, it
followeth

followeth no more, then if one, should argue; *King Henry the eight and his adherents in schisme deuiding them selues from their lawfull Pastors, were no true Church*; Ergo *English Catholickes liuing in perfect obedience to the Vicar of Christ cannot be truelie a Church*; or to this : *The soule and body separated can make no true man.* Ergo *if they be conioyned they can make no true man.*

But better may we say, that this is a doughty comparison. For, in the first *enthymeme* F. K. argueth from positiue and sinfull separation from lawfull Bishops, to mere negatiue and faultlesse want of vnion with a particuler Bishop: and also from positiue diuision from Bishop both particular and vniuersall, to positiue vnion with the vniuersall Bishop. For Henry the eight and his adherents were positiuely and sinfully deuided both from particular and

vni-

vniuerfall Bishop ; and therefore
were neither a particuler Church,
nor yet parts of the vniuerfall
Church; whereas English Catholicks were meerly negatiuely deuided from a particular Bishop, becaufe they had none, and that
without their fault; and were po-
fitiuely vnited to the vniuerfall
Bishop, wherby they were parts or
mēbers of the Catholick Church.
But this vnion with the vniuerfall
Bishop did not make them a particuler Church, but only a part of the
vniuerfall Church. And as it is more
to be a particuler Church, then
onelie to be a part of the vniuerfall
Church, fo more is required to
make a particuler Church, then
to make a part of the vniuerfall
Church. And as the vniuerfall
Church is *Plebs Epifcopo vniuerfali
adunata*, a people vnited to the
vniuerfall Bishop : fo a particuler
Church

Church is *Plebs Episcopo particulari adunata,* a people vnited to a particuler Bishop. But F. K. seemeth to think, that onely positiue and sinfull separation from a Bishop, such as was in King Henry the eight and in Schismatikes, maketh no Church, whereas mere want of vnion maketh no Church; because a Church is a people positiuely vnivnited to a Bishop, as is euident by those words *Plebs sacerdoti adunata.* And consequently the want of this positiue vnion, whether it be by mere want of vnion, or by positiue separatiõ, maketh a Non-Church. And F. K. his second enthymeme hath the like fault, for not onely positiue separation of a soule from a body, maketh it to be no man, but also mere want of vnion to a body; as if God should create a soule by it self.

Neither doth the vnion of Catholiks

tholiks with the vniuerſall Biſhop make them a formall particular Church, more thē the vniõ of Iriſh men to the King of England doth make them a particular kingdome Their vnion to our King would make them good ſubiectes, but not a particular kingdome, without vnion to him as particular King of that kingdome: as our vnion to the Pope would make vs good Catholiks, but not a particular Church, vnleſſe he either were, not onely our vniuerſall Biſhop, but alſo our particular Biſhop, or els ſhould giue vs ſome particular Biſhop.

Will F. K. Say that it is all one to be a parte of the vniuerſall Church, and to be a particular Church? to be part of a great Empire and to be a particular kingdome? if no, then let him tell how a particular Church, can be without a particular Biſhop, more then
a par-

a particular kingdome or Principa-
litie, without a particular King or
Prince.

Quæst. 1. §. 12: *p.* 7. he saieth *D.*
Kellison against all good Logike, and as
it may seeme, against prudence proueth
his conclusion by Principles more harsh
then the conclusion, as the necessitie of
a Bishop in England, because it is de
iure diuino *that euerie such particular*
Church should haue a Bishop. That
without a Bishop it cannot be a parti-
cular Church. That vnlesse euerie parti-
cular Church haue a Bishop the vniuer-
sall should not be a Hierarchie composed
of diuers Churches. That without a
Bishop we *cannot haue Confirmation,*
which who wanteth, *Saieth D. Kelli-*
son, is no perfect Christian.

But it rather seemeth that F. K.
neuer knew good Logik. For, good
Logik teacheth that there is *Duplex*
notius; nobis & natura; and that the
best proofs are *ex notioribus natura,*
(for,

(for, *scire*, *est per causam cognoscere*)
which vsually are not *ex notoribus nobis*, as causes are lesse knowne to vs, then the effects. And all those proofs of *D. Kellison* are *Ex causis*. For, *Ius diuinum* is a cause why a Bishop is necessarie. The not being of a particular Church without a Bishop is a cause, why it should haue a Bishop. That the vniuersall Church is not *integraliter* a *Hierarchie*, vnlesse euerie notable parte thereof be a particular Church, is cause why euerie particular should haue a Bishop, as the lamenesse of a man, vnlesse all his notable parts should be entier. The want of vndoubted Confirmation without a Bishop (because manie graue Deuines, and that vpon no light reasons, deny that the Pope can giue Priests leaue to confirme) is a Iust cause to haue a Bishop. That who wanteth Confirmation, according

to

to the generall doctrine of the fathers and deuines (as partely is alreadie, and partlie shall hereafter be more fully shewed) is no *perfect Christian*, is a iust cause to haue a Bishop, who onely can giue vndoubted Confirmation. And who proueth the necessitie of a Bishop in England by these causes as *D. Kellison* doth, bringeth the best kinde of proofs that Logike teacheth. And thus much for a tast of F. K. his skill in Logik, and in arguing.

Section VII.

That F. K. changeth the question.

THE question betweene *D. Kellison*, and F. K. is whether England, or English Catholiks

were

were a particuler Church before it
had a particuler Bishop. The Doctor deineth that it was: F. K. affir-
meth the contrary, becaufe, faieth
he, The Pope may be both vniuerfall Bishop of the Catholike
Church, and particuler B. of England, as *Leo I X.* was of *Tull.*

But either he argueth, *A poſſe, ad
eſſe,* or chaungeth the queſtion. For
if he proue that the Pope heretofore was particuler Bishop of En-
glãd, becauſe he may be, he argueth
à poſſe ad eſſe. If he make the queſtion what may be, he chaungeth it.
For, the queſtion was not what the
Pope may be, but what he was: and
his example maketh rather againſt
him felfe; both becaufe it is a fin-
gular example, and therefore one
might rather fay ; No Pope was
Bishop of a particuler Church out
of Rome, but onely Leo IX. *Ergo*
there was none of England; as alſo

** ſo h
qu. 2
§. 10
& 11
Item
§. 13
pag.21
Item
§.16.
p. 29.
Item
qu. 3.
§. 6.
p. 38,*

C   becaufe

k Ba-
roni⁹
Anno
1049.
Voluit
dum
vixit
dici
Tul-
lensis
Epis-
copus.

becaufe * Leo IX. kept the title of
the Church of Tull, and neuer Pope
yet held the title of the Church of
England. More ouer both Gregory
XV. and Vrban VIII. in their Breues to the two Bishops of *Chalcedon*
fay, that the Catholikes of England wanted the commodities
which other Catholikes get by
their Bishops ; and therefore fent
the Bishop of *Chalcedon* to fupply
their wants, *ergo* thefe two *Popes* did
not think that English Catholike
had any particuler Bishop, or els
they thought he did not doe his
duety.

Likewife he chaungeth the queftion in this, that whereas the queftion was only of the neceffity of a
particuler Bishop to make a particuler Church, F. K. changeth it to
a diftinct Bishop from all others,
faying *qu. 2. §. 10. p. 23. Ergo euery
Church need not haue it owne particuler*
diftinct

diſtinct Biſhop : as if becauſe **D.** *Kelli-ſon* required a particuler Biſhop to make a particuler Church, there-fore he required a Biſhop diſtinct both from the vniuerſall Biſhop, or from other particuler Biſhops: or had denied that the Pope being vniuerſall Biſhop, could be alſo a particuler Biſhop, or a Biſhop, that is a Biſhop of one dioceſe could not be Biſhop of an other alſo. As if, for, example, becauſe a particuler Earle is required to a particuler Earledo̅, Therefore the *King of England* can-not be *Earle of Cheſter*; or one Earle haue twoe Earledoms ; no King twoe kingdoms, and the like. Thus to chaunge the queſtion vpon igno-rance, is groſſe, and to chaunge it wittingly, is worſe; and argueth the weakneſſe of his cauſe, which for-ceth him to chaunge it.

An other queſtion is , *whether feare of perſecution be ſufficient to re-*

C 2 *fuſe*

fuse a Bishop, *or the Sacrament of Confirmation*, as appeareth by these words of *Doctor Kellison*, related by F.K. *q.* 4. §. 12. *p.* 76. *I am of opinion, that a particuler Church cannot except any long time against hauing a Bishop for feare of persecution.* Item: *I think neither any country, nor any one of the country for feare of persecution can oppose against the comming of a Bishop, though thereby the onely Sacrament of Confirmation should be wanting.* In which words, the case is putt onely of *feare of persecution in generall.* Nay F.K. §. 16. *p.* 85. relateth these words of *D. Kellison* c. 14. nu. 9. *Euery man in particuler cannot be comdemned of sinne for omitting confirmation for feare of loosing his life, lands, and liberty.* And yet F. K. in the same §. *p.* 83. saieth: *Our case is when confirmation cannot be had without hazard of goods, libertie, and life.* And q. 3. §. 5. pag. 37. *To affirme as M. D. doth, that it is* de

iure

iure diuino *to haue a particular Bishop in England*, *and not onely that there is such a precept*, *but moreouer*, *that no persecution can excuse the obligation thereof*, *or giue sufficient cause of dispensation* (*all which he most proue, if he will speake whome*) *is a paradox*, *to speake sparingly*. And yet immediatly before *pag.* 83. *cit.* he saied of *D. Kellison: what good dealing this is, I leaue to the censure of an vnpartiall Reader*: which he saied because *D. Kellison* citing *Clements* words, that one is no *perfect Christian* without confirmation, added not these, *Si non necessitate sed incuria sic aut voluntate remanserit.* And yet the very same words did *Canisius* omitt in the text of his Catechisme cap. 5. de Confir. without censure, that I know, of any Catholik. And I hope F. K. will not be the first that will censure his brother *Canisius*.

But better may I say, what good

dea-

dealing is this of F. K. to change the case *from feare of persecution in generall, to hazard of life, lands and libertie*, when as *D. Kellison* (as himselfe confesseth) doth professe not to bind any in such hazard. And if one should say that English Catholiks may not refuse the hauing of a Priests for Confessiõ, and other Sacraments for feare of persecution: would F. K. change the case, and say *our case is of hauing Priests with hazard of goods libertie and life*: in which case he would hardly proue, that Catholiks were bound to haue Priests: and what good dealing this were, to chaunge the question of hauing Priests, I leaue to the Censure of F. K. himselfe: and if he would not account this good dealing in question of necessitie of Priests, and of Confession, why shall we account it good in the question of Bishops and of Confirmation? *He*

Section VIII.

He Claweth the English Catholiks, and yet saieth they are not worth noting.

Q Vast. 2. §. q. p. 18. he saieth the most zealous Catholiks of England, who for their vnion with the Sea Apostolike, constancie in profession of their faith, ioyfull Suffering, losse of goods, libertie & life, haue beene a spectacle in the sight of God and his Angells, and admirable to the eies of men. Yet qu. 3. §. 7. p. 38. he denieth the Church of England to be a notable parte of the Church. For thus he speaketh: *If we consider the multitude of Catholiks* (in England) *which alone make a true Church, we shall find*

C 4 *it to*

it to be more then farre from a great, or notable part of the Catholike Church spread ouer the whole world. Are English Catholiks who are moſt zealous, gratious in the ſight of God and Angells, admirable in the eyes of men, farre from being a notable parte of the Catholike Church? Nay what part of the Catholike Church is more notable then ſuch? If one would ſay that F. K. his order were not a notable parte of the Church, he would not take it well: and yet is it farre from being ſo great a part as the Catholikes of England are.

He

Section IX.

He resisteth episcopall autho-
ritie meerely vpon hu-
mane motiues, and yet
putteth not downe his true
humane motiue.

QVast. 7. §. 3. p. 183. he auou-
cheth that *D. Kellison* wrote
his doctrine, *vpon humane designe,* and
qu. 1. §. 9 pag. 6. It cannot be pleasing to
almightie God to treat of holy things
vpon particuler designe and humane
respects. And yet doth he and his
Abettors resist the introducing of
Episcopall authoritie in England,
and the Sacrament of Confirmation vpon no other motiue, then
feare of persecution, medling with
wills, disposing of pious legacies,

C 5   as is

as is to be seene *qu.* 7. §.13. But the true humane motiue *F. Rudesind* discouered in his *Mandatum Sect.* 7. *pag.*171. *Least Regulars should by comparison of the Clergy, grow contemptible with the laitie.* And *p.* 172. *Least they should be excluded from the almes, by which they haue hitherto beene mantained.* And the same motiues discouer the *Three Regulars* in their letter to the Bishop of *Chalcedon.* For, §. 1. they say, that the Bishop *would by degrees make the Regulars contemptible, and depriue them of the fruits of their labours by which they subsist.* Which reason they repeat againe *§. vlt.* Which is plainely enough to confesse, that they resist Episcopall authoritie for pride, least thereby they should become contemptible; and for couetousnesse, least thereby they should leese some of their almes.

And that pride and ambition was
the

the motiue, why *Iesuits* oppoſed
Epiſcopall dignitie, *F. Rudeſind* in
publik letters written to the *Con-*
gregation. de propaganda fide. 22. De-
cemb. 1624. in the name of his
whole Congregation teſtifieth in
theſe words: *Rogamus ergo nos Bene-*
dictini &c. We Benedictines your
humble ſeruants and children requeſt,
that reiecting their accuſations who
diſgrace the good name of the beſt
Prieſts, onelie that they alone may
shine, as it were, by antiperiſtaſis, a-
mongſt a headleſſe Clergie, that they
may ſeeme to be of the Hierarchie, and
by diuiſion of minds in the clergie do
thinke to make themſelues the beſt way
to their greatneſſe; you would vouch-
ſafe to graunt a Bishop to England,
ſeeing no prouince of the Chriſtian world
hath more need; whether we conſider
the neceſſitie of the Sacrament of Con-
fimation, or agreement and concord of
Eccleſiaſticall diſcipline, which ſeemeth
C 6   *can*

can by no meanes be kept without Episcopall authoritie. Neither ought Regulars to feare, lest Episcopall authoritie
should be burdensome to them, because
authoritie instituted by Christ, can hurt
no true Christian. And of the persons
of *D. Kellison*, and *D. Smith* in particular he thus writeth in the same
letter: *Coram Deo* &c. *I call God to
wittnesse, that they are held in so great
veneration, both by us, and almost all
the Catholiks of England, both for in-
tegritie of life and excellencie of Doctrine, that we thinke scarce any can
be found equall to them, much lesse surpasse them, in all the Clergie, Secular
or Regular.* And after much commendation of them he addeth: *San-
cte affirmamus* &c. *We religiously
auouch, that what we haue testified
of the saied Doctors are things so manifest
to all good men in England, that surely
they will suffer a great scandall, whosoeuer shall heare that they are sham-*
lesly

lesly calumniated before your tribunall.

Thus he in the yeare 1624. both of the chief motiue vpõ which the Iesuits resisted Episcopall authoritie, to wit, that they might florish among a headlesse Clergie, and that they might seeme to be *Hierarches*, and make way to their greatnesse; and likewise of the necessitie of Episcopall dignitie both for *Confirmation*, and for concord, and for discipline, which can no way be kept without Episcopall authoritie; which also he saieth, Regulars ought not to feare as burdensome to them, because authoritie instituted by *Christ* cannot be hurtfull to any true Christian; And finally he taketh, as it were, on oath of the vertue and learning of *D. Kellison*, and *D. Smith*. And protesteth that all good men wilbe highly scandalized to heare them ill spoken of.

But

But how differently within lesse then 3. yeares, both he and his, haue both printed, written, and spoken, both of episcopall authority, and of *D. Smith* now Bishop of *Chalcedon* his person, onelie becaufe he required of Regulars to aske his Approbation, is to to manifeft. And is it poffible, that the onelie matter of Approbation should thus in fo short a time alter mens iudgement, both of Epifcopall authority, and of the Bishops person? But the iudicious Reader who confidereth, that this letter was written by the Monkes vpon no paffion, and confirmed by oaths, and that what they haue written fince, hath proceeded from offence conceaued about Approbatio, will foone fee to whether of *F. Rudefinds* writings, he ought rather to giue credit. And thus much be fpokē by occafion of F.K. his affertion that *D. Kellifon* wrote

his

his doctrine *vpon humane designe*: which the reader will indge by what hath bene saied already, how much more truely it may be retorted vpon F. K. him self, and his complices.

Section X.

That F. K. openeth a way to banish all Priests both secular and Regular out of England.

Passionat men many times are so earnest to hurt their aduersaries, that they do not mark what hurt with all they do to themselues: which befalleth to F. K. who vpon desire to bannish a Bishop out of England, maketh a way to driue out all Priests. For the chief cause why

he

he would not haue Catholiks to
admit of a Bishop, is feare, that
thereby their perfecution would be
encreafed: which no leffe, yea farre
more, maketh againft Priefts. For
who is ignorant, that there are
moft feuere lawes againft Priefts,
and none againft Bishops? That the
comming in of *Seminary Priefts* did
incenfe the ftate vnder *Q. Elizabeth*
to augment the perfecution, who
hoping that with the death of *Q.*
Maries Priefts, Catholike Religion
would die in England, but feeing
afterward them felues fruftrate of
that hope by the coming in of Seminarie Priefts, were more feuere.
But who doubteth, but that feue-
ritie was much encreafed by the
coming in afterwards of the Iefuits
and by the publick chalenge made
by *F. Campian,* and the writings of
F. Parfons againft the Earle of Le-
cefter? For prefentlie after came
forth

forth proclamations againſt *Ieſuits*
and *Seminarie Prieſts*, and bloody
lawes were enacted againſt them,
and their harbourers or mantai-
ners, which had not beene before.
And yet for all this, Catholikes at
that time, did not write or ſpeake
againſt the cōming in of *Seminary
Prieſts and Ieſuits*, but were rather
glad of their cōming, though they
had, for the preſent, help by *Q. Maries Prieſts*.

But if F. K. call to minde, how
beſides the terrible lawes enacted
againſt receiuers of Ieſuits into
their howſes, many Catholikes
haue ſuffered much damage in
their goodes and libertie, and ſome
in their liues, and how euen ſome
families haue alſo beene almoſt
quite ruinated, I thinke he will be
aſhamed to goe about to baniſh
a Biſhop vpon meere pretended
feare of encreaſe of perſecution.

And

And now when after 8. yeares,
since Episcopall authoritie came
into England, there hath beene no
lawes made, no persecution raised
againstCatholikes,no man endaun-
gered by occasion of Episcopall authority, yet must it needs be banished out of England vpon pretence (for sooth) of danger to Catholiks, though indeed it be (*as F.
Rudesind wrote*) onelie that they
them selues may domineere and
Shine amongst a headlesse Clergy,
and so make way for their owne
greatnesse.

But they will say perhaps, that
without Priests men can haue no
Sacraments, which although it be
not true,if it be vnderstood of euery
Sacrament,seeing without Priests
baptisme and matrimony may be
had : nor any way true, if it be vnderstood of simple Priests , seeing
that

that all the Sacraments which can
be had by Priests, may be had alſo
by Bishops, and more to: and as
ſome write in the beginning of the
Church, all Prieſts were alſo
Bishops: Yet ſuppoſe it were true,
how will they prooue, that men
are bound to receaue the Sacraměts
in danger of loſſe of goods, liberty
and life, as by the lawes they are, in
receauing any English Prieſt into
their houſe? Why may they not
abſtaine from Sacraments in ſuch
danger, or why may not ſome could
Catholikes ſay of receauing Prieſts
and of confeſſion, as F. K. doth
quæſt. 4. p. 76. Til he heare, that the
contrary is void of probability, Catho-
likes are ſure they may with a ſafe con-
ſcience keep their goods, liberty, and
lifes, for ſome more neceſſary occaſion.
At leaſt why may they not rather
ſeek for forraine Prieſts, then ad-
uenture with English Prieſts, as F.
K. would

K. would haue them to feek for
a forraine Bishop rather then an
English; and yet is there no law,
ancient or new, made againft a
Bishop, as Bishop, but onely as he is
Prieft.

The good which a Bishop can
bring to Englād is farre greater. For
he can adminifter the fame Sacraments which Priefts can, and two
greate Sacraments more ; he *[can
make Catholikes perfect Chriftians, he can gouerne them, and
preferue Ecclefiafticall difcipline,
which is fo neceffary, as for it *S.
Thomas 3. p. qu. 65. art. 4.* with the
confent of all deuines, faieth that
Order is *neceffarie neceßitate medÿ*
to the Church, which he proueth
out of that. Prouerb. 11. *VVhere
there is no gouernour the people will
fall*. The good which may come
to Catholikes by Epifcopall authority is fpirituall, eternall, great,
certaine,

certaine, and prefent; The danger
which can be pretended by it, is
worldly, temporall, future, vncertaine? It was inftituted by Chrift;
appointed by the holy Ghoft for
the gouernmente of the Church.
The power, by which it was fent
hither, fupreme on earth, irrefra-
gable; The deliberation, by which
it was concluded, graue, mature,
and of long time. The approouers
and acceptors of it in England, the
farre greateft and moft obediente
part: The example, of other Catholikes both in Holland and Ireland
to be imitated: The admiffion required of fuch authority, not formall, or pofitiue, but onely tacite,
by not refifting it, as was before
Approbation began to be mooued
to the Regulares: The oppofers of
it, men, who in plaine words difcrie
their owne, and their fellowes pri-
uat and temporall intereft.

Befides,

Besides, as F. K. *qu. 4. §. 7 .*faieth of finne, fo fay I of lawfull authority, *when the danger is neither* proximum, *imminent , and fuch as morally* will *not be auoided, or els not of any determinate time, perfon, or place, but onely in generall, a common* wealth *may tolerate fuch a ftate for obtaining a greater good* . And if a common wealth may tolerat fuch a ftate, why not much more Catholikes tolerate a deuine authority, inftituted by God, and appointed in England by his Vicar on earth for their exceeding great good, if they will make vfe thereof , feeing there is no imminent danger, and fuch as cannot be morally auoided, or of any determinat time , perfon or place; but at moft in generall, that can come therby ? And againe I fay with F. K. *loc. cit. Catholikes are not obliged for auoiding of fome remote , and vncertaine, voluntary danger of a few*

few to depriue them selues of present, certaine and great spirituall
commodities, of excessiue encrease
of grace in this world, and glory in
the next.

F. K. saieth *qu. 5. §. 9. p. 106. In
the businesse of our saluation , euery
addition to true and not presumptuouse
hope ought to be greatlie esteemed.* And
*§. 2. p. 149. It is a case worthy to be
deplored with many teares, that in
wordly and temporall affaires men
will vse their vttermost diligence, and
emploie all their wittes for compaßing
such poore ends, with all poßible securitie; and yet in the maine bußinesse of
our soule, we are willing to find out
anie seeming probabilitie.* And I add,
that it is farre more to be deplored
that *Regulars* who professe perfection, and to incite men not onelie
to procure their saluation with all
poßible securitie, and to frequent
the Sacraments, euen out of necessitie

fitie, but alfo to endeauour to perfection, should be their Captaines
and Ringleaders to find out excufes
not to receaue *Confirmation*, which
maketh perfect Chriftians, giueth
fpirituall grace and ftrength to endure perfecution; and to reiect Ecclefiafticall iurifdiction: which, as
F. Parfons faieth in his anfwere to
S.Ed.Cookes fift book of Reports, giueth
life, vertue, force, and efficacie, to
euerie Religion, and, is the onelie fure
guide to faluation.

Moreouer *qu. 5. §. 28. p. 153. he*
faieth to auert men from Religion can-
not be free from a great finne, especiallie
if it be ioyned with some diminution of
the perfection of religious state in ge-
nerall. And can it be free from a
great finne, to auert men from obedience to *Episcopall authoritie*, especiallie if it be ioyned with some diminution of the perfection of Epifcopall ftate in generall. And as he
addeth

addeth *ibid.* §. 31. *p.* 160. *that vnleſſe the cauſe be very ſufficient, all ſuch diſpenſation* (in vow of Religion) *can ſerue onelie to ſend a man to hell with a kind of quiet conſcience,* ſo I add, that all excuſe of diſobedience to *Epiſcopall authoritie,* if it be not very ſufficient, can ſerue onely to ſend a man to hell with a kind of quiet conſcience and ſeeming ſecuritie.

Finally I conclude with thoſe words of his *ibid.* §. 32. *p.* 161. *On their behalf I wish, they may in this buſineſſe ſo proceed, that when the true colour of things shall begin to appeare by the light of an approching future life, they may haue no iuſt cauſe to frame a different iudgment, and fill their ſoules with other wishes* (touching Epiſcopall authority) *then at this preſent they doe.*

D   CON-

THE
CONCLVSION.

IN the end of this Pamphlet the Author saieth: *he wished that rather then he should vtter any thing in diminution of charitie, in disparagement of sacred episcopall dignitie, in preiudice of the common good of Catholikes, almightie God would forbidde his pen to cast inke, and if that were not enough, benumb his right hand.* But he needed not require a miracle to hinder him from writing such a pamphlet, who rather should haue feared, least that might befall him, which we see, hath happened already,

already to two of the chiefest
writers against the *Episcopall authority of the Bishop of Chalcedon.* Yet by
this it cleerly appeareth, that he
was not without some feare of
scruple of conscience to write that
he did, knowing no doubt, (not-
withstanding this verball protesta-
tion of his desire to the contrary)
that he doth diminish charity, dis-
parage sacred Episcopall dignity,
and consequently preiudice the
common good of Catholikes not a
little by this kind of scandalous
writing:

And he concludeth, that *how
soeuer Regulars may by some be
esteemed to oppose for their owne ends
the hauing of a Bishop in England, or
some authority by him chalenged, yet
he would most willingly spend his
blood for the purchasing of times sutable
with the enioying of a Catholik Bishop
endowed with as much authority, as*
any

any *particuler Bishop*, *in the whole Church of God*. But that *His Order* hath opposed *Episcopall authoritie* from time to time for their owne ends , we haue already heard the testimony of the whole *Congregation* of the *English Benedictines*, and we haue also their owne confession, both by words and deeds. And the most which the Author wisheth in this place, is, that he might haue calme and peaceable times: hoping perhaps, that such times would by meanes of other cōmodities, which they would bring to his *Order*, counteruaile tēporall losses which he feareth by *Episcopall authority* in these times ; and therefore these times he accounteth not sutable to enioy a Bishop; as if Christ had appointed Bishops onelie for calme and peaceable times, and not *Omnibus diebus vsque ad consummationem sæculi, donec occurramus omnes in vnitatem*

tatem fidei ; or not especially for
times of persecution to confirme
their Brethren, to direct and encourage them in their spirituall con-
flicts , as a Generall is especially
needfull to an armie in time of
warre, a Pilot to a ship in time
of tempest, a Pastor to a flocke in
time of wolues.

He will haue those who are but
Cooperators or Coadiutors of Pastors ; and them also instituted by
the Church (as *Missionarie Regulars*
are) necessarie to England in time
of persecution, and Bishops, who
are the proper Pastors of soules, instituted by the holy Ghost to gouerne the Church , placed by God
for the Consummation of Saints,
that they be not carried away with
euerie winde of false doctrine, to be
sutable onely in time of calme.
What is this but in effect to say that

D 3   man

man is wiser then God? Mans in-
ftitution for time of perfecution, is
to be preferred before Gods inftitu-
tion? Man knoweth what kinde of
perfons are more fit for the Church
in time of perfecution, then God? Is
this nothing in difparagement of
Sacred Episcopall dignitie, and preiudice of the common good of Catholikes?

Vaine it is to wish for miracles
to hinder you from writing in difparagement of *Episcopall dignitie*
and preiudice of the common good
of Catholikes? Whileft you will
iudge nothing to be fuch, which
you apprehend may be fome difparagement, or temporall preiudice
to your owne *Order.* I may fay vnto
you, as *Moyses* faied to thē that op-
pofed the firft Bishops, that were in
the Church vnder the law: *Multum*
erigimini filij Leui; Ye do much exalt
your

your selfes ye sonnes of Leui. Or as *Saint Paul* saied to some: *An à vobis pro-* cessit verbum Dei? *Or did the worde of God proceede from you?* As it did from the Apostles, who were Bishops? Teach not, I pray you, Christ and the holie Ghost, what times are su-table for Bishops: teach not them, who are fittest for the Church in time of persecution: fright not Ca-tholikes with your preteded feares of persecution, which none of them, noe nor your selues, pre-tended here, till you feared *Appro-bation:* till then, both you, and the Lay Catholikes, that adhere vnto you, could both welcome and in-uite the Bishop to their houses: but the requiring of *Approbation* hath made him dreadfull and hatefull; Surely not to Lay Catholikes, for whose good *Approbation* was ex-acted, but to you, who thereby

feared

1. Co c. 14.

feared the diminution of your credits with the laity, and some other temporall losse. If this feare of yours were ended all feare of persecution in the Lay Catholikes would soone be at an end. But Christ our Sauiour, who hath promised to be with the first Bishops and their successors; *Omnibus diebus vsque ad consummationem saculi*, will (I doubt not) assist Episcopall authoritie in England, will not suffer this poore afflicted Church to be depriued of so great an ornament, and so great a good vpon meere humane, temporall, future, generall, and vncertaine pretended feares, which with much more apparence might be preteded against that *Regular Order*, which most opposeth this most lawfull, most sacred, most profitable, most necessarie, Ordinarie authoritie of Bishops, from which all

all prieſtly function, all Sacraments, and all authoritie to admi-
niſter them, or the word of God,
and in one word, all ſpirituall goods
in Gods Church, as from their
proper fountaine, next after God, do
flow and proceed.

SAINT BONAVENTURE
The Psalter of the B. Virgin Mary
1624

THE
PSALTER
OF THE
B. VIRGIN
MARY.

Conteyning many deuout
Prayers & Petitions.

Composed in the French Tongue by a
Father of Society of IESVS.

And
Tranflated into Englifh by
R. F.

Permiffu Superiorū M DC. XXIIII.

2

TO THE

RIGHT HONOVRABLE

AND VERTVOVS

LADY, THE LA.

Cecily Compton.

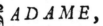 *ADAME,*

This little , but
golden Booke, com-
mĕ̄ded both by the Patronage

A 2   of

of one of greateſt *Queenes*
in *Europe* (to whome it was
firſt preſented in *French*
Attyre) and by the generall
approbation of the better
ſort of *Catholiques*, I now
ſend vnto your *Ladiſhippe*
cloathed in *English* garments: which how it will become it I know not, nor dare
promiſe any thing more,
then my fidelity in the Trã-
ſlation, & my ſingular affection in the dedication of it.
VVhich I beſeech you, *Ma-*
dame,

dame, fauourably to accept,
as the first & choicest fruite
(in this kind)of my tyme,&
that liberty for the which
your Ladiship was once so
Noble, and timely an In-
tercessour, untill I may further imploy it, in the search
of some more ample subiect,
wherby I may expresse my
selfe so by your singularVer-
tue gayned (which none can
know but they must honour,
none heare but they must admire) and by your Fauour

A 3   obliged

*obliged (which hath byn so
great towards me, as I neuer
had ambition to wish for
greater) that I shall sooner
dye, then not liue your Ladi-
ships euery way*

Most gratefully deuoted

R. F.

THE

THE
PSALTER
OF THE
B. VIRGIN MARY.

The Authors Preface.

HE Royall Pro-
phet *Dauid*, in
the depth of
his afflictions, & in the

A 4   height

height of his felicity, ac-
knowledging God to be
the foueraigne Author
of all things, vfed continually to conuert him-
felfe vnto him, and euen
plunge his Heart into
the profound medita-
tions of the beaefits ,
which he had receaued
from his liberall hand,
who from the lowest
degree of a filly sheep-
heard, had exalted him
to the highest throne of.

Royall

Royall maiesty, and to the gouernement of a people the most deare vnto him of all other Nations.

Vpon which occasion that he might shew himselfe gratefull, and be made worthy to receaue still more of his benefits, he composed in his praise certaine Praiers which he called *Psalmes*, for that either he himselfe did singe

A 5　　them

them to his Harpe, or caused them to be sunge by his ordinary singers, with a most profound, & deuout grauity.

This deuotion of holy *Dauid* beinge very acceptable vnto god, his posterity was very carefull to collect all that he composed in this kind And hauing, euen out of darkenes & forgetfulnes gathered to the number of an hundred and fifty

of

of his Praiers, by meanes
of the happy memory
of *Esdras* , they called
them *The Psalter* .

Since which time in
imitation thereof , as
piety increased amonge
the Christians , diuers
holy Fathers haue made
Canticles , & Psalmes,
aswell in the honour of
our Lord Iesus Christ,as
of the blessed Virgin
Mary his mother: out of
which I haue gathered

the

the best and deuoutest
Praiers addressed vnto
that most sacred Queene
ioyning them together
in this little ensuing
Booke, & do call it, *The*
Psalter of the Virgin Mary.

And as that of *Dauid*
conteineth an hundred
and fifty *Psalmes* ; so
doth this in like man-
ner conteine a hundred
& fifty most deuout Sa-
lutations, which are de-
uided into fifteene Peti-
tions,

tions; and to euery petition at the beginning is put down the Churches Angelicall Salutation, to implore the fauour and aide of the said sacred Virgin : and in the end thereof, is added likewise a Hymne composed in her honour.

You may begin your Psalter then in this manner. After that you haue deuoutly in a modest manner composed your
selfe

felfe, before an Image
of the Bleffed Virgin, or
otherwife in any deuout
place, or Oratory, lif-
ting vp your hart and
thoughts to that moft
glorious Queene, be-
fore euery petition fay,
the *Aue Maria*, in En-
glish, or Latin, as fol-
loweth.

THE

THE FIRST
PETITION.

Aue Maria gratia plena Dominus
tecū, benedicta tu in mulieribus,
& benedictus fructus ventris tui
IESVS. Sancta Maria mater Dei,
ora pro nobis peccatoribus, nunc
& in hora mortis nostræ. Amen.

Mary, Mary, Mary,	
Mary, Mary, Mary,	
Mary, Mary, Mary,	
Mary, Mary, Mary,	Most Blessed Virgin
Mary, Mary, Mary,	Mary, mo-
Mary, Mary, Mary,	ther of
Mary, Mary, Mary,	God pray;
Mary, Mary, Mary,	for me.
Mary, Mary, Mary,	
Mary, Mary, Mary,	

O

O GLORIOVS Virgin Mary surpassing in grace all women in the world, who haue bene most pleasinge to God, and onely found worthy to beare in your sacred wombe his Blessed sonne I E S V S, & to be chosen as his spouse, to recompence the fault committed by *Adam*, and *Eue*, our first Parents; Grant me grace, that I may receaue pardon
for

for my finnes; & that your deare fonne, & my Sauiour IESVS may look vpon me with the eyes of his mercy, and not of his iuftice.

2. Draw neare vnto me, O moft Bleffed Virgin who are the mother of the Afflicted My enemies are gathered togeather againft me, and I haue this onely refuge, to caft my felfe vnder the shaddow of your

wings.

wings. Defēd me against
their enterprifes , and
bring them all to shame
and confufion .

Shew vnto me the
faire beames of your
countenance; powre out
vpon me your mercy,
with the which you re-
plenish the whol world:
for I know that thofe
who haue recourfe vnto
you , are alwaies heard,
and that you doe pitti-
fully regard the affli-
&ed,

éted, from that high
feat of your glory.

3. Help & remedy the
infirmity, which ouer-
whelmeth me, and the
dolour which oppref-
feth my heart: and per-
mit me not to be as a
prey vnto mine ene-
mies, nor that they may
fay of me: He is fallen
into our nets, he shall
be our prey, & thofe in
whō he trufted shall not
be able to deliuer him.

O

4. O most sacred Virgin, change my sorrowfull plaints and teares, into sweet ioy and consolation, to the end that my tongue may alwaies blesse you, & sing forth your praises for euer.

Your Maiesty and Greatnes, together with the incredible sweetnes of your infinite Mercy, haue obliged my lipps to publish the praises of no other, then of your

selfe

selfe: be you glorified (O most amiable Virgin) together with your sweet sonne Iesvs, both now and euermore. Giue my soule entrance into Paradise whē it shall leaue my body, and by your holy praiers deliuer me frō the dreadfull paines of hell; and let all that which is due vnto me for my sinnes, be cancelled by your merits.

5. I haue put my hope

and

and confidence in you,
and to you now I onely
addreſſe my Praiers ,
knowing full well that
I am moſt vnworthy to
be heard by your deareſt
ſonne; yet by your inter-
ceſſion I truſt my petitions will be granted .

Let your face shine
& ſend forth its beames
vpon the clouds of my
ſinnes; and let the ardent
zeale of your Charity
melt, and diſſolue the

cold

cold ice of my slouth &
negligence, that I may
presently rise and con-
fesse my selfe vnto you,
and by you aske pardon
and forgiuenes of your
Blessed Sonne, for my
sinnes.

6. Present my vowes
& praiers (O B. Virgin
refuge of sinners) before
the Maiesty of your sonne
I esvs : Be a media-
tresse for me vnto him,
that he may not so

much

much regard what I
haue done againſt him,
as what he ſuffered for
me, and for all mankind
vpon the tree of the
Croſſe.

You haue bene the
cauſe (O holy Virgin)
that God , tooke hu-
mane fleſh vpon him; &
that being come to ſaue
vs , he hath bin made
our brother , and in all
things like to vs. except
in ſinne. You then as a

mother

mother can obtaine for vs all that which we aske him.

He hath made you to be borne without any spot of originall sinne, that you might be the instrument of our saluation : and hauing made his Tabernacle in the middest of your sacred Breast, he will pardon vs for the loue of you, and not iudge vs according to his Iustice, but

B   accor-

according to his mercy.

7. Remember our humanity (O sweet Virgin) and the dolours which you haue suffred in this world ; & grant that we may find Grace with you, who are the foundresse of our grace and saluation.

Grant, that inioying your presence I may be rauished in the Cōtemplation of the beauty of your Countenance,

which

which the Angels neuer ceafe to admire ; & that the paines and forrowes which I haue fuffered in my body , may be eafed with a fweet and quiet repofe of mind.

8. Stretch forth your hand (O moft benigne Virgin) to draw me out of the filthines of my finnes; and let the great-nes of your mercy blot out the multitude of my offences , fupplying by

B 2　　　your

your merits what in iu-
ſtice I dare not demaund
of your ſweet Sonne I E-
S V S. Your Eies are ac-
cuſtomed to regard with
pitty the poore & affli-
cted, of which number I
am one.

9. Turne not therfore
your face away from me,
(O mercifull Virgin)for
I put my truſt in you, &
haue called vpon you
from my infancy.

The feaſt daies of your

solem-

folemnity which are ce-
lebrated by the Church,
haue bene thofe of my
greateft ioy: and when I
haue meditated on your
natiuity, my foule hath
reioyced with it felfe, as
the birdes do at the ri-
finge of the funne, and
with them I haue funge,
and lifted vp my voice,
afloon as I awaked from
my fleepe.

10. Glory be to you
(O facred Virgin) whom

I will beare in my heart
all the daies of my life, to
put me in mind that you
are shee who haue borne
IESVS CHRIST the Au-
thour of our saluation,
and do reigne with him
in euerlasting blisse, and
happinesse.

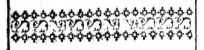

THE

THE HYMNE
Fletus Longæui.

THe Kinge of kings when he did see
    The greatnes of our misery,
To Anne a winged Herald sent,
    Who thus declared his intent.
Doe you reioyce & do not feare,
    For you behould, a child shall beare,
Although your yeares doe yt deny,
    And make you thinke it cannot be.
The mother of the world so great,
    Shall of your bloud, deuoyd of heat,
Conceiued be, and in you breed,
    Though hardly to be credited.

Nor scarse can it beleeued be,
How woudrous great this child
shall be :
Whose glorious praise , and wondrous
worth,
For euer shall be sounded forth.
Ioachim ouer-ioyd was made,
When by the Angell it was said ,
That of Saint Anne so weake and old
The mother of god begotten should.
To you all glory be therfore
IESVS, that Blessed Virgin bore:
To God the Father Lord of might ,
And to the holy Paraclite .

THE

THE SECOND
PETITION.

Aue Maria gratia plena Dominus tecū, benedicta tu in mulieribus, & benedictus fructus ventris.tui I E S·V S. Sancta Maria mater Dei, ora pro nobis &c.

Mary, Mary,	Blessed Mary most immaculate Virgin, and Mother, pray for me.

I Beseech you(O most louing Virgin)to cast on me your sweet & pittifull eye, and help me that I may worke the saluation of my soule, to the end that after its separation from my body, it may ascend streight vnto you, in the Celestiall glory.

Grant that I may see your resplendant face crowned with twelue stars, and your glorious

body

body inuironed with the light of the sunne , as with a rich and costly garment , soe shall I be comforted and delighted to my harts content.

You are the Sanctuary , into which I desire to retire , and free my selfe frō the captiuity of mine enemy: for I know well, that by you , the head of the serpent hath byn bruised, and that all his enterprises & indea-

uours,

uours, compared with your power, are weak and feeble.

2. Thofe who turne towards you in all their actions (as the needle touched with the Adamant turns toward the North wherfoeuer it be fet) shall neuer miffe of the right way, but at the end of their life shall ariue fafely at the port of your holy fauours & graces.

It

It is yow that are the Tower built vpon the firme ground, through which God came vnto man, & man ascends to God: & you are she that are exalted into heauen aboue all the Quires of Angells, & Cherubims.

I also magnify you as the foūdresse of Grace, and springe of saluatiō, since that it is you who haue repaired the whole world, fallen from the

glory

glory of heauen, & haue
put it into the right way
whereby it may returne
thither againe.

3. I will neuer ceafe to
befeech you with all my
defires & affections, vn-
till that by my Praiers I
haue obtaind your holy
benediction, and by the
effects therof know that
yow haue beheld me
with côpafsion, & giuen
eare vnto my Praier.

It is not in the fauour

of

of men, neither in Kings
nor Princes, that I haue
put my hope, since that
to rely on them is vaine;
but it is in you (O holy
Virgin Mary) who neuer
forsake those that call
vpon you.

4. I will humble my
heart before you, for I
know that the proud
shall not be entertained
neare vnto your sacred
maiesty, since the glory
of Earth hath nothing

to doe with that of Heauen. Those places are for the poore of spirit, for those who are pure and cleane of hearte, for those who are mild and peaceable, and for those who daily weepe, lamenting with true contritiō their sinnes & offences

All you Infidells, & wicked liuers, whome Pride hath puffed vp, shall goe and burst your selues in the profound

depth

depth of hell, there to be tormēted, & laughed to scorne for euer: but this Holy Virgin will stretch out her hand vnto vs, becaufe we haue wholy put our truft in her; and she will turne away from vs the indignation of her Bleffed fonne Chrift IESVS.

She hath borne him in her moft facred and chaft wombe, & by shewinge vnto him thofe

breſts

brests which he hath su-
cked so téderly, she will
appeafe his anger & in-
dignation againſt vs ,
who haue ſo many waies
tranſgreſſed his Com-
mandements .

5. If you (O ſacred
Virgin) do not vnder-
take our defence , how
shall we doe to appeare
before him ? Seing that
aſloone as he was borne,
the Princes and Poten-
tates of the earth came
                    from

from farre Countries to adore him, & submitted themselues to his power.

Put words into my mouth (O Blessed Virgin)that I may worthily praise you,since the heauens théselues set forth your glory ,and that all creatures call vpon you, when they are oppressed with daunger and affliction.

6. (O Blessed Virgin) most ready to aide vs, I

know

know, that affoone as
you haue fauourably ex-
tended your hand vpon
the ficke, they are pre-
fently healed; and that
the waues of this trou-
blefome fea are foone
appeafed by your Com-
mandement.

I haue feene the Vo-
tiue tables of thofe who
haue bene deliuered by
your interceffion, han-
ging vp in your Chur-
ches and Oratoryes, in

memory

memory thereof, as so many Trophies of your Wonders.

7. You are that sweet Rose by whose odour the dead are raised to life; & the faire lilly of your face hath made the king of heauen enamoured on you, whome among all others he hath cho-sen to be the mother of his onely Sonne.

You haue had inclosed within your breast him,

whom

who all the world could
not containe, & he who
weilds the fame with his
hand, would be borne
of you, clothinge him-
felfe with our infirme
humanity, within your
facred & virginall wōbe.

I will reioyce at your
vertue and power, and
the fweetnes of your
Name shal fill my foule
with confolatiō: neither
will I ceafe to praife and
exalt you with Hymnes,

Pfalmes,

Psalmes, and Canticles, but day by day will *I* render vnto you my vowes.

8 Giue vnto me (O most Blessed Virgin, true wisedome, by the which I may be enlightened to know alwaies the truth, that I may not be of the number of those, who walke astray out of the right path.

Grant this vnto me (O most chast Virgin) that

that I may resist the pleasures and desires of carnall Concupiscence, which my aduersary stirs vp in me, to the end that the light of grace may come and lodge in my heart, and there send forth resplédant beames of vertue, as longe as I shall liue.

9. Keepe me in the perseuerance of well doinge, & put such a bóud vnto my lipps, that they

may

may be hardned againſt
euill words; & lift vp my
thoughts in that máner
vnto you, that they may
not defcéd to any vaine
and earthly cogitations.

If tribulations aſſaile
me, be ready (O Bleſſed
Virgin) to ſuccour me,
and turne your pittifull
face towards me, who do
preſent my humble re-
queſt, and praiers vnto
you. Do not abandon me
at the houre of death,

C   when

when myne enemy will prepare to lay all his fnares, and practife his wily deceits, to preuaile a-gainft me, to plunge me into defpaire, by prefen-ting before myn eies the enormity of my finnes.

10. Receaue my foule (O Bleffed Virgin) into your hãds, when it shall haue left this mortall body, and take it into your protection, for it will be loft with feare, &

will

will not know to what
side to turne, to saue it
selfe, vnles vnder the
shaddow of your mercy.

Vndertake I beseech
you my cause, when it
shall appeare before the
tribunall of the great
Iudge, and moderate the
sentence, by appeasinge
and pleasinge him, that
by your meanes I may
obtaine pardon and re-
mission of all my sinnes.

Obteine for me by

C 2   your

your grace and merci-
full bounty, a place of
perpetuall habitation,
amonge those who be in
paradise, there to enioy
happily that felicity
which the soules of
those who haue deuout-
ly serued you, doe eter-
nally possesse.

THE

THE HYMNE

A solis ortus cardine.

FRom the Risinge of the sunne,
  Vnto the place of his retorne,
Let Christ our Princes praise be sunge
  Of holy Mary Virgin borne.
The maker blest of all, we see
  A seruile corps on him did take,
That those he made, lost might not be,
  And flesh by flesh he free might
    make.
The heauenly grace did enter free
  Into his chastest mothers wombe,

C 3   And

And there that wonder wrought, which shee
    Did scarcely know, how it could come.
That breastes pure closure straight was made
    Gods Temple of most sacred worth,
And which man neuer touched had,
    The eternall Word a sonne brought forth.
The Quire celestiall did reioyce,
    The Angels vnto God did singe,
And to the sheepheards sent a voice
    The maker great of euery thinge.
All glory euer be to you
    Sweet IESVS, Blessed Maries sonne,
The like vnto the Father too,
    And holy Ghost, whilst ages runne.

THE

THE THIRD
PETITION.

Aue Maria gratia plena Dominus
tecũ, benedicta tu in mulieribus,
& benedictus fructus ventris tui
I E S V S. Sancta Maria mater Dei,
ora pro nobis *&c.*

Mary, Mary, Mary,
Mary, Mary, Mary,
Mary, Mary, Mary,
Mary, Mary, Mary,
Mary, Mary, Mary,
Mary, Mary, Mary,
Mary, Mary, Mary,
Mary, Mary, Mary,
Mary, Mary, Mary,
Mary, Mary, Mary, } Most Blessed amonge all vvomen, pray for me.

O BLESSED Virgin Mary Mother of vnlimited power, adored, and called vpon by the Vniuerfe, giue me ftrength to refift the tentations of my inuifible enemies, and let them fall into the fnares, that themfelues haue layed for me. Arme & ftrengthé me againft my felfe, for that I feele an inward repugnance from doing good, and am farre more

incli-

inclined to thinke, speake, and do euill, then to practise good, and vertuous workes.

2. Be alwaies neere vnto me (O Glorious Virgin)that the cleare beames of your deuine aspect, may keepe me from abandoninge my selfe to euill; since my ghostly Enemy seekes nothinge more, then to lead me into the depth, and darkenes of sinne.

C 5   He)

He will not dare to
behould your mercifull
face, for he who is moſt
hideous and fearefull,
cannot ſupport your ce-
leſtiall beauty : & as for
me, I will put my ſelfe
vnder your feet, implo-
ringe your mercy and
ayde. I will lift vp my
voice vnto you, becauſe
I haue put my hope in
your grace, and by your
merits & interceſſion, I
truſt to find your ſonne
Chriſt

Chriſt Iesvs well plea-
ſed with me .

3. Take me into your
protection(moſt Bleſſed
Virgin) shewing me the
true pathes of vertue ,
by which I may paſſe the
pilgrymage of this life,
and be my guide , and
conduct to the kinge-
dome of heauen.

My Refuge is in you
alone , and aſſoone as I
knew what it was to
loue , I dedicated my

selfe to you, who haue
wholy wonne & gained
my heart: wherefore I
will euer praise, & exalt
your merits & deserts.

O Virgin most excel-
lent in all perfections, &
perfect in all excellen-
cyes, you are she who
haue alone amonge all
women bene found wor-
thy to be the Mother of
Christ Iesvs, God, and
Sauiour of the world

4. I know that you
haue

haue bene exiled & ba-
nished with him, ther-
by to teach me, that
my naturall Country is
to be with him and you,
and that I muſt fly the
company of the wicked,
if I deſire to follow his,
and your footſteps.

You are adorned with
all beauty & filled with
all heauenly graces; for
the ſplendour of the
Sunne doth crowne your
head with his beames,

and

and the shining of the
Moone, giues light vnto
your feet.

You are more excel-
lently faire, thē pretious
stones : and their shi-
ninge luster looseth its
grace, compared to the
beames of your celestiall
light.

5. The stars of heauen
borrow all the excellen-
cy that they haue from
you, and your sides haue
bene the tabernacle and

san-

sanctuary of God, whose pleasure it was to be at once your Creator, and your Sonne.

We haue good reason to exalt you aboue all the celestiall and terre-stiall Creatures, since you are become the Lad-der of Iacob, by which we ascéd vnto the glory of God, into his heauen-ly paradise.

You are the flaminge bush that Moyses saw,

which

which neuertheles was
not confumed ; for al-
though you were both
mother and daughter
of our Sauiour IESVS
Chrift, yet your Virgi-
nity hath byn deuinely
prefcrued.

6. You are the Arke
of Noë, who haue faued
the world frō that moft
dangerous deluge of the
temptations of Sathan,
and haue fet free the
poore captiued crea-
tures,

tures, from his infupportable tyranny.

You are likewife the Doue, which brought the branch of Oliue, in figne that the water of dolour was dried vp: the Rod of Aaron, the fleece of Gedeon, & the Iuory throne of Salomon are prefiguratiue Emblems of your Excellency.

It is you, that haue made amendes for the fault of our firft parent

Adam,

Adam, and haue reco-
uered by humility, that
which he loſt by pride
and preſumption ; for
that of you is borne the
Redeemer of humane
Generation.

7. The ſerpent to his
ruine & perdition hath
proued your force, for
vnder your feet his head
hath bene bruized, and
his forces haue byn al-
together diſſipated, and
brought to nothing.

It

It is you whom the Auncient Patriarcks so much desired to see before they died, and of whome the Prophets in their wrytings haue made so often, & honourable mention.

You are she who was to proceede from the Royall line of Dauid, & beare the Messias promised in the Law, & who gaue the holy Fathers in Limbo soe great cause

of

of ioy , when S. Iohn Baptiſt announced vnto them the newes that Chriſt was borne of you.

8. Heauen , Earth, the Sea , and all Creatures do likewiſe bleſſe and praiſe eternally the memory of your moſt holy and ſacred Name: and as for me who haue lifted vp my voyce vnto you, when I was oppreſ- ſed with tribulation , if you should haue for-

ſaken

faken me, to whō should
I haue then repayred,
that would haue looked
vpon me with pitty and
compaſſion?

Doe not forſake me
(O Virgin of admirable
ſweetnes ;) and let not
mine enemies haue oc-
caſion to ſay by moc-
king me : He hath ho-
ped in her in vaine, ſince
that now behould he is
vnder our power.

I will offer vnto you

a ſa-

a sacrifice of praise with
all humility and deuo-
tion,& réder my vowes
at the Altars erected in
your honour, & where
you often worke your
miracles.

9. O most holy Vir-
gin, giue vnto all those
who deuoutly inuocate
you,the vertue to put in
execution their good
purposes & holy desires,
to the end that the ef-
fects may turne to your

glory,

glory, and the ſaluation of their owne ſoules.

Incline your eies to behold vs with pitty, let your eares be open and attentiue to our ſupplicaſions, and your mouth ready to intercede for vs, to your Bleſſed ſonne Chriſt Iesvs.

Let your hands be ready to ayd vs when we ſhall be aſſaulted by any tribulation, or aduerſity.

Dry

Dry vp the sorrowfull teares, which our eies haue so longe time powred out, and despise not our praiers; since that on you alone we rely, and in all our afflictions do turne our selues to you.

10. I will go and prostrate my selfe vpon the earth in the Churches & Oratoryes dedicated to your honour, & there will I go seeke for the comfort which I hope

from

frō you, for I haue seene the great miracles which your hands haue done, and haue bene rauished with the admiration of the magnificence of your Altars.

I will confesse your Name amonge all Nations, because it is holy, & will tell vnto strange people the wonders of workes; and will make knowne to all, the Maiesty of your greatnes.

D   THE

THE HYMNE
Quem terra, pontus.

He whom the Earth, the sea, & sky
   Worship, adore, & magnify,
And doth this threefold engine steare,
   Maries pure Closet now doth beare,
Whom Sunne, and Moone, and Crea-
   tures all,
   Seruing at times, obey his call,
Powring from heauen his sacred grace,
   I'th Virgins bowels hath tane place.
Mother most blest by such a dower,
   Whose maker, Lord of highest
   power,

VVho

Who this wide world in hand con-
    taines ,
  In thy wombes Arke himselfe re-
    straines .
Blest by a message from heauen brought,
  Fertile, with holy Ghost full fraught,
Of Nations the desired Kinge,
  Within thy sacred wombe doth
    springe.
Lord may thy Glory still endure,
  Who borne wast of a Virgin pure,
The Fathers, and the spirits of loue,
  Which endles worlds may not re-
    moue.

D 2   THE

THE FOVRTH
PETITION.

Aue Maria gratia plena Dominus tecũ, benedicta tu in mulieribus, & benedictus fructus ventris tui I E S V S. Sancta Maria mater Dei, ora pro nobis &c.

Mary,	Mary,	Mary,	
Mary,	Mary,	Mary,	
Mary,	Mary,	Mary,	
Mary,	Mary,	Mary,	Most Blessed Mary, Refuge of all sinners pray for me.
Mary,	Mary,	Mary,	
Mary,	Mary,	Mary,	
Mary,	Mary,	Mary,	
Mary,	Mary,	Mary,	
Mary,	Mary,	Mary,	
Mary,	Mary,	Mary,	

O

OBLESSED Virgin Mary, whose light is more resplendāt then the light of the Sunne and Moone, enlighten my soule interiourly with the beames of your Grace, that the darknes of sinne may be driuen from thence, and that I may follow the doctrine of Christ Iesus your sonne, who euen in his younge yeares, did teach the most learned

in

in the Temple.

2. Giue me grace to ferue you in all holynes and iuftice , accompaninge my vowes, with fuch chaftity & purity, as may be pleafing and acceptable before your face.

Make me to know the ioyes of Paradife, by the fplendour of your glory, to the end that my defire to be there , may encourage me more and more

to piety and deuotion,
and to the obſeruing of
the commandements of
God.

3. Who shall lead me
into your Tabernacles
(O moſt Benigne Vir-
gin) if I be bereft of the
light of your grace? how
shall I dare to haue re-
courſe vnto you, if once
in all my life I haue not
deuotly inuocated your
holy name; & if by my
praiers I haue not made

my selfe knowne vnto you?

I haue almost lost my selfe in the night of this world, & ther hath bene none but you to assist me, and with the wicked I was become wicked. I haue heard the senseles and the foolish say in their hearts : They put their trust in a woman, but she shall not deliuer them. Make them say vntruly (O sacred Vir-

gin)

gin) and proue them to be lyers , taking vengeance of the iniury, that they do vnto you.

4. The Serpent hath sought to cast man out of the tabernacle of God, & hath filled his mouth with lyes, to seduce him by the perswasions of a woman , and to banish him with himselfe from the kingdome of heauen for euer : But he hath laboured in vaine, for

D 5   he

he must render himselfe
subiect to a woman; since
that by the fruit of your
wombe , his power hath
bene ouercome, and the
gates of his kingdome
haue bin made desolate,
crushed , and turned in-
to dust .

5. Arise (O Virgin)
and by vertue of your
stronge Arme resist his
indeauours . He is al-
ready confounded in
himselfe , not knowinge

by

by what meanes you did
bringe forth a Sonne,
and yet preserued your
virginity vnspotted. He
hath bene like the fish,
who vnder the bayte of
the humane body of
your sonne our Sauiour,
hath swallowed thehoke
of his owne death, and
ruine

He hath made a pit
that we might fall into
it, hauing cunningly de-
ceyued our first mother;

but himselfe is fallen thereinto, & you our second mother farre more wise and aduised, haue bruized his head

Call to mynd the iniury that he would haue done you, and defend my cause against him; for you are the aduocate of poore sinners, who put their hope and trust in your intercession.

6. Stirre vp your fury against your enemies,

and

and let then learne, to
their coſt, not to deryde
and ſcorne at you, or
your miracles; for their
tounge is too ready to
detract your Name.

Make others afraid
by the exemplar ven-
geance of thoſe, whom
you ſo chaſtice; and re-
new now the meruailes
of your miracles, with
which you haue here-
tofore filled all the corners of the Earth.

I

I haue seene the Gul-
fes open vnder the feet
of the wicked who haue
blasphemed against you,
and the signes of their
impiety haue bene as a
flame, to increase the fire
of my loue towards you,
and redouble my hatred
to their abhominations.

7. Make the sweet stre-
ames of your graces to
spring within me, since
that you are the foun-
taine of all sweetnes, of

which

which the Creatour of the world hath desired to drinke, suckinge the milke of your Sacred breasts.

You are the Vessel of Election wherein hath bene put the treasure of all treasures and the fairest Iewell of the world; for he whome you haue borne, hath framed and moulded the world betwixt his fingers, and ballance ith as he pleaseth

by the force of his right
hand.

8. Obtaine for me of
your deare sonne IESVS,
true light that I may fall
no more, but be streng-
thened in my fayth a-
gainst all entisements of
those who enter not into
their synagogues but by
the gates of lyinge and
impiety; And haue no
other word more fre-
quent in their mouthes,
then blasphemy against

your

your holy Name.

I beseech you (O most
mercifull mother) that I
may safely passe the wa-
ues of tribulation in this
life, for you are the An-
ker of my hope, desiring
to arriue to you, who are
the Porte of my safety.

You are the Refuge
of sinners, and by you
they find remission of
their offences: I am the
greatest, and most grei-
uous amõg them; looke

vpon

vpon me in pitty, and
make my ſpirit to repoſe
in peace, vpon the firme
ſtone which is IESVS
Chriſt our Lord.

9. Be vnto me as a
ſtrong Bulwarke, againſt
the face of myne ene-
myes, & appeare vnto
thē fearefull as a ſtronge
Army in array, ready to
aſſaile them.

You comfort all thoſe
that are oppreſſed with
ſorrow and anguiſhe of

mind

mind, and giue confola-
tion to thofe who weep,
& lament: I haue bene
long time troubled and
vexed: put once an end
vnto my dolours, and
afflictions.

My frendes, being
fréds of the world, haue
turned away from me in
my afflictions, euē thofe
who liued, and did eat
with me: I haue not bene
fupported but by the af-
fiftance of your fauours,

like

like as an Orphane left
by his Father, and Mo-
ther vnto mifery.

10. Recount (O yee
Heauens) all the mer-
uailes that you fee of
this Bleffed Virgin , and
with your cõtinuall mo-
tions praife her; and you
the morning Star exalt
her glóry. Let all thofe
who fhall fee your fer-
uour, lift vp ther voyces
with you vnto heauen,
for they fhall bleffe her,

and

and singe Hymnes to her glory and honour.

Reioyce (O Queene of heauen) for all Nations shall call you Blessed; & the Angels themselues, which are with you, shall fill the firmament with your praises, and you shall be exalted euen vnto the throne of the diuine Maiesty, in the presence of the Patriarches, Prophets, & of all the Saints .

THE

THE HYMNE

Ductus per virginem.

*S*Weet IESVS to Ierusalem
 The Virgin with her forth did
 beare,
Vnto a feast they kept solemne
 At the returne of euery yeare.
But when the day orepast, and shee
 Now ready for to make returne,
She left alone, and lost was he,
 Nor what to doe she knew, but
 mourne,
She asked for him all about,
 And in the presse of people sought:

       But

But he in tender yeares went out,
　　And Rabbins in the temple taught.
And there the law of Moyses, he
　　At twelue yeares old, so treated on,
As with profound Deuinity
　　He fild their spirits euery one.
But full of ioy the Virgin was
　　When she vnto him neere did draw,
Findinge her sonne in such a place,
　　And in such deep dispute him saw.
All glory euer be to you
　　Sweet IESV, Blessed Maries sonne,
The like vnto the Father too,
　　And holy Ghost, whilst ages runne,

THE

THE FIFTH
PETITION

Aue Maria gratia plena Dominus
tecú, benedicta tu in mulieribus,
& benedictus fructus ventris tui
IESVS. Sancta Maria mater Dei,
ora pro nobis &c.

Mary, Mary, Mary,	
Mary, Mary, Mary,	
Mary, Mary, Mary,	Most Blesled Mary,
Mary, Mary, Mary,	Comfortresse of
Mary, Mary, Mary,	the Afflicted, pray
Mary, Mary, Mary,	for me.
Mary, Mary, Mary,	
Mary, Mary, Mary,	
Mary, Mary, Mary,	
Mary, Mary, Mary,	

I WILL retyre my selfe vnto you (O most Blessed Virgin) vnder the shaddow of your Mercy : for those who trust in you, do find consolation, and you neuer forsake the afflicted who call vpon you.

Grant me grace, that I may imitate your holy conuersation, taking example by your Charity, Humility, & other your rare vertues, which

E   haue

haue rendred your life
admirable to all thofe,
whofe eyes of faith are
open to know, and fee
them.

2. Haue care (O Blef-
fed Virgin) of my foule
that it thinke of no-
thinge which is not ho-
ly; & let my tongue be
mute, when it would
fpeake ill of my neigh-
bour.

Make blind mine eyes
in feeing the pleafures

&

& delights of the world, that by their faire shew they may not intice me to follow them, and in the end cast my Soule headlonge into perdition.

Conduct my feete in the true path of vertue, that they may not stumble at vices; and beinge once freed from iniquity, I may enioy the beatitude which I hope for in heauen.

3. Enlighten the blind-
nes & ignorance of my
foule with the beames of
the Grace of the Holy
Ghoſt , who defcended
vpon you, at the inſtant
when you cōceiued our
Bleſſed Sauiour IESVS
Chriſt, & whé you were
prefent with the Apo-
ſtles on Whitfunday.

Make me performe my
duty in my vocation to
your contentment and
my faluation, that I may

praife

praise you, and set forth
your worth; & that my
mouth may be alwaies
occupyed in singinge
forth your merits.

4. O all you Nations
who haue tasted of the
bountifulnes of her be-
nefits, and to whom she
hath prepared the way
of saluation by her most
desired childbirth, ma-
gnify with me, this glo-
rious Virgin Queene.

Haue recourse vnto

E 3   her

her in your afflictions,
for she goeth about the
whole world to know
the playnts of those who
be afflicted, & helpeth
them readily when they
call vpon her sacred
Name.

Praise her daily for her
great Humility, which
hath bene the occasion
that Christ Iesus would
take humane flesh in
her wombe, and humble
himselfe vnder her Ma

ternall

ternall authority.

5. Praise the Excellency of her beauty, which hath not byn any thing diminished; & the fairenes of her face, which hath euer flourished as the faire Lyllie of the springe.

Lift vp her honour to the Heauens, for she hath bene exalted aboue all the Angels, & placed in the throne and feate of the Maiesty of God,

E 4   there

there to be adored, as the Queene of heauen, eternally.

This is the Virgin sprunge from the Roote of Iesse, who brought forth the fruit of our Saluation, & hath made a Brotherly league betweene God and Man.

6. O most bountifull Virgin, we see on euery side of vs the signes of your holy magnificéce, and the earth is euery

where

where filled with your miracles.

Yow côfort the afflicted, you help the lame, you giue fight to the blind, you reftore the madde to their fenfes, you raife vp the dead to make knowne their innocency, and you put food into the handes of the poore & needy.

7. The euill fpirits are chafed away by the Inuocation of your Name,

and

and diuers by your aid
haue byn recouered out
of the fearefull clawes
of the diuell, and freed
from the paines of hell.

Thofe whō you haue
healed from diuers and
innumerable difeafes, are
the trūpets which found
out, vnder the vault of
this Vniuerfe, the incre-
dible Effectes of your
power; & the memory
of them shall be engra-
uen for euer in the foules

of

of the liuing.

The Churches wher-
in your Name is inuoca-
ted, shall be seen filled
with Treasures, offred
vnto you by vowes; and
the Vessels consecrated
to your seruice shall surpasse in beauty, all the
pretious Iewels and Ri-
ches of the Temple of
Salomon.

8. O sacred Virgin,
help also my corporall
necessities as I shal need

for the good of my
soule, and not for any
desire to possesse great
riches; for I had rather
haue a little with your
grace, then all the world
without it.

Returne (O my soule)
with all thy affections
towards this sea of Mer-
cy, who doth vse to lend
a fauourable eare to the
poore that perseuere in
singinge forth her prai-
ses, and who do im-

portune

and let then learne, to their coſt, not to deryde and ſcorne at you, or your miracles; for their tounge is too ready to detract your Name.

Make others afraid by the exemplar vengeance of thoſe, whom you ſo chaſtice; and renew now the meruailes of your miracles, with which you haue heretofore filled all the corners of the Earth.

I

I haue seene the Gul-
fes open vnder the feet
of the wicked who haue
blasphemed against you,
and the signes of their
impiety haue bene as a
flame, to increase the fire
of my loue towards you,
and redouble my hatred
to their abhominations.

7. Make the sweet stre-
ames of your graces to
spring within me, since
that you are the foun-
taine of all sweetnes, of

which

which the Creatour of
the world hath desired
to drinke, suckinge the
milke of your Sacred
breasts.

You are the Vessel of
Election wherein hath
bene put the treasure of
all treasures and the fairest Iewell of the world;
for he whome you haue
borne, hath framed and
moulded the world bet-
wixt his fingers, and ballance ith as he pleaseth

by

by the force of his right hand.

8. Obtaine for me of your deare sonne IESVS, true light that I may fall no more, but be strengthened in my fayth against all entisements of those who enter not into their synagogues but by the gates of lyinge and impiety; And haue no other word more frequent in their mouthes, then blasphemy against

your

your holy Name.

I beseech you (O most mercifull mother) that I may safely passe the waues of tribulation in this life, for you are the Anker of my hope, desiring to arriue to you, who are the Porte of my safety.

You are the Refuge of sinners, and by you they find remission of their offences: I am the greatest, and most greiuous amōg them; looke

vpon

vpon me in pitty, and make my ſpirit to repoſe in peace, vpon the firme ſtone which is IESVS Chriſt our Lord.

9. Be vnto me as a ſtrong Bulwarke, againſt the face of myne ene-myes, & appeare vnto thē fearefull as a ſtronge Army in array, ready to aſſaile them.

You comfort all thoſe that are oppreſſed with ſorrow and anguiſhe of

mind

mind , and giue confola-
tion to thofe who weep,
& lament : I haue bene
long time troubled and
vexed : put once an end
vnto my dolours, and
afflictions .

My frendes , being
fréds of the world, haue
turned away from me in
my afflictions, euē thofe
who liued , and did eat
with me: I haue not bene
fupported but by the af-
fiftance of your fauours,

like

like as an Orphane left
by his Father, and Mo-
ther vnto misery.

10. Recount (O yee
Heauens) all the mer-
uailes that you see of
this Blessed Virgin , and
with your cõtinuall mo-
tions praise her; and you
the morning Star exalt
her glóry. Let all those
who shall see your fer-
uour, lift vp ther voyces
with you vnto heauen,
for they shall blesse her,

and

and singe Hymnes to her glory and honour.

Reioyce (O Queene of heauen) for all Nations shall call you Blessed; & the Angels themselues, which are with you, shall fill the firmament with your praises, and you shall be exalted euen vnto the throne of the diuine Maiesty, in the presence of the Patriarches, Prophets, & of all the Saints.

THE

THE HYMNE

Ductus per virginem.

Sweet IESVS to Ierusalem
  The Virgin with her forth did
  beare,
Vnto a feast they kept solemne
  At the returne of euery yeare.
But when the day orepast, and shee
  Now ready for to make returne,
She left alone, and lost was he,
  Nor what to doe she knew, but
  mourne,
She asked for him all about,
  And in the presse of people sought:

But

But he in tender yeares went out,
  And Rabbins in the temple taught.
And there the law of Moyses, he
  At twelue yeares old, so treated on,
As with profound Deuinity
  He fild their spirits euery one.
But full of ioy the Virgin was
  When she vnto him neere did draw,
Findinge her sonne in such a place,
  And in such deep dispute him saw.
All glory euer be to you
  Sweet IESV, Blessed Maries sonne,
The like vnto the Father too,
  And holy Ghost, whilst ages runne,

THE

THE FIFTH
PETITION

Aue Maria gratia plena Dominus
tecū, benedicta tu in mulieribus,
& benedictus fructus ventris tui
IESVS. Sancta Maria mater Dei,
ora pro nobis &a.

| Mary, Mary, Mary, |
| Mary, Mary, Mary, |
| Mary, Mary, Mary, |
| Mary, Mary, Mary, |
| Mary, Mary, Mary, |
| Mary, Mary, Mary, |
| Mary, Mary, Mary, |
| Mary, Mary, Mary, |
| Mary, Mary, Mary, |
| Mary, Mary, Mary, |

Most Bles-
led Mary,
Comfor-
tresse of
the Affli-
cted, pray
for me.

I WILL retyre my selfe vnto you (O most Blessed Virgin) vnder the shaddow of your Mercy : for those who trust in you, do find consolation, and you neuer forsake the afflicted who call vpon you.

Grant me grace, that I may imitate your holy conuersation, taking example by your Charity, Humility, & other your rare vertues, which

E   haue

haue rendred your life admirable to all those, whose eyes of faith are open to know, and see them.

2. Haue care (O Blessed Virgin) of my soule that it thinke of nothinge which is not holy; & let my tongue be mute, when it would speake ill of my neighbour.

Make blind mine eyes in seeing the pleasures

&

& delights of the world,
that by their faire shew
they may not intice me
to follow them, and in
the end caſt my Soule
headlonge into perdi-
tion.

Conduct my feete in
the true path of vertue,
that they may not ſtum-
ble at vices; and beinge
once freed from iniqui-
ty, I may enioy the bea-
titude which I hope for
in heauen.

3. Enlighten the blind-
nes & ignorance of my
soule with the beames of
the Grace of the Holy
Ghost , who descended
vpon you, at the instant
when you côceiued our
Blessed Sauiour IESVS
Christ, & whê you were
present with the Apo-
stles on Whitsunday.

Make me performe my
duty in my vocation to
your contentment and
my saluation, that I may

praise

praise you, and set forth
your worth; & that my
mouth may be alwaies
occupyed in singinge
forth your merits.

4. O all you Nations
who haue tasted of the
bountifulnes of her be-
nefits, and to whom she
hath prepared the way
of saluation by her most
desired childbirth, ma-
gnify with me, this glo-
rious Virgin Queene.

Haue recourse vnto

E 3   her

her in your afflictions, for she goeth about the whole world to know the playnts of those who be afflicted, & helpeth them readily when they call vpon her sacred Name.

Praise her daily for her great Humility, which hath bene the occasion that Christ Iesus would take humane flesh in her wombe, and humble himselfe vnder her Ma

ternall

ternall authority.

5. Praise the Excellency of her beauty, which hath not byn any thing diminished; & the fairenes of her face, which hath euer flourished as the faire Lyllie of the springe.

Lift vp her honour to the Heauens, for she hath bene exalted aboue all the Angels, & placed in the throne and seate of the Maiesty of God,

E 4   there

there to be adored, as
the Queene of heauen,
eternally.

This is the Virgin
sprunge from the Roote
of Iesse, who brought
forth the fruit of our
Saluation, & hath made
a Brotherly league bet-
weene God and Man.

6. O most bountifull
Virgin, we see on euery
side of vs the signes of
your holy magnificēce,
and the earth is euery

where

where filled with your
miracles.

Yow cōfort the affli-
cted, you help the lame,
you giue fight to the
blind , you reſtore the
madde to their ſenſes,
you raiſe vp the dead to
make knowne their in-
nocency , and you put
food into the handes of
the poore & needy.

7. The euill ſpirits are
chaſed away by the In-
uocation of your Name,

E 5   and

and diuers by your aid
haue byn recouered out
of the fearefull clawes
of the diuell , and freed
from the paines of hell.

Those whō you haue
healed from diuers and
innumerable diseases, are
the trūpets which sound
out, vnder the vault of
this Vniuerse, the incre-
dible Effectes of your
power; & the memory
of them shall be engra-
uen for euer in the soules

of

of the liuing.

The Churches wher-
in your Name is inuoca-
ted, shall be seen filled
with Treasures, offred
vnto you by vowes; and
the Vessels consecrated
to your seruice shall surpasse in beauty, all the
pretious Iewels and Ri-
ches of the Temple of
Salomon.

8. O sacred Virgin,
help also my corporall
necessities as I shal need

for the good of my
soule, and not for any
desire to possesse great
riches; for I had rather
haue a little with ycur
grace, then all the world
without it.

Returne(O my soule)
with all thy affections
towards this sea of Mer-
cy, who doth vse to lend
a fauourable eare to the
poore that perseuere in
singinge forth her prai-
ses, and who do im-

portune

portune her with their
Praiers.

9. I will loue this Vir-
gin, and I will haue per-
petuall ioy in my heart:
But you (O yee wicked
men) who detract from
her holy Name , will
feele the punishement,
and fall into the depth
of Hell, if you conuert
not your selues speedily
vnto her.

She easily pardoneth
the offences committed

against

againſt her; wherefore I
will caſt my ſelfe vnder
her feet, thereby to ob-
taine grace, and pardon
for the ſinns that I haue
committed in not ſer-
uinge her.

I beſeech you (O Great
Queene of heauen, and
Lady of the Angels) to
purify my heart with
the fire of your loue and
charity, that laying aſi
de all other earthly af-
fections, it may mount

vp

vp vnto you in heauen, by praier & meditation.

10. Illuminate my foule, that it may not be caft afleepe, in the foulenes of finne; and that it may neuer ceafe, (beinge ftrengthened by your Fauour) to render thankes vnto you.

I defire to pray vnto you, & to inuocate you more & more, that therby I may be taken into your protection, & put

out)

out of danger of falling
againe into the hands of
myn enemyes, for amōg
them there is no com-
paſſion, but all manner
of confuſion.

Praiſed by your holy
Name, & let the honour
which is due vnto you
be publiſhed among all
Nations, ſince that from
your ſacred wombe iſ-
ſued the ſunne of Iuſtice
Chriſt IESVS.

THE

THE HYMNE
Virgo Dei genitrix.

O Fruitfull Virgin, who within
    Your sacred loynes could carry him,
Whom the Earths so large extend
    Neuer yet could comprehend.
Of your most purest bloud was made
    That body in which he was clad,
Whose faith and constant sufferance
    From sinne is our deliuerance.
You both together Mother are,
    And yet a Virgin passing rare:
Who when we into danger fall,
    You ready are to helpe vs all.

To

To you all Nations are inclind,
  Succour assured there to find.
For your blest hand doth giue redresse
  To euery one that's in distresse.
To you all glory be therefore
  Sweet IESV, *that the Virgin bore:*
To God the Father Lord of might,
  And to the holy Paraclite.

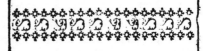

THE

THE SIXT
PETITION.

Aue Maria gratia plena Dominus
tecū, benedicta tu in mulieribus,
& benedictus fructus ventris tui
IESVS. Sancta Maria mater Dei,
ora pro nobis &c.

Mary,	Mary,	Mary,
Mary,	Mary,	Mary,
Mary,	Mary,	Mary,
Mary,	Mary,	Mary,
Mary,	Mary,	Mary,
Mary,	Mary,	Mary,
Mary,	Mary,	Mary,
Mary,	Mary,	Mary,
Mary,	Mary,	Mary,
Mary,	Mary,	Mary,

Most Blessed Virgin Mary, the Cause of our Ioy, pray for vs.

O

O MOST holy Virgin Mary, who are exalted to greater, and more excellent authority then any other creature, giue me grace to feare, and honour you, to the end, that I may not defile my soule in the finke of finne.

As longe as I shall feare to finne, and belieue that you are present euery where, & that you do fee me if I commit

my soul
of sin

to sin
Belieue
present
do see

mit any offence, I shall
be hindred therby from
putting any euill inten-
tion in execution.

2. A Vassaile dare not
presume to commit any
thinge before his Lord,
that may displease him;
neither shall I, who take
you for my Lady and
Mistresse, dare to do any
thing that may be con-
trary to your cōmand
before your face.

I desire that my soule

depend

depend, & be subiect to you, because that your precepts & documents are good, & very easy to be kept; and the tribulation that it suffers for your loue, is very great.

3. Deliuer it from dāger (O holy Virgin)and cleanse it from all sinne, that it may appeare faire before the face of Christ IESVS your Beloued sonne; and that he may bestow his graces vpon

it,

it, in turninge his eyes
of mercy and compaſ-
ſion towards it.

Giue ioy and gladnes
to my ſpirit, ſince that of
longe time tribulation
hath enuironed me, and
ſought to oppreſſe me
in a moment, that ſo I
might not haue recourſe
to you.

I am one of the Chil-
dren of Adam, who haue
bene loſt, and incurred
the curſe, for diſobeyng
God,

God; but I will repaire that euill, by obayinge you, that I may thereby become one of the children of God.

His will shall be written in my heart, therby to force me to accomplish the same, and you (O Gratious Virgin) will aide me with your grace, without which I cannot long perseuere.

4 My forces are weake to doe good, and stronge

to

to do euill; wherefore I
haue need that you be
alwaies neere vnto me:
for I know that you will
excite me to the one, &
caufe me fly the other.

Let the fweet liquour
of your grace, ftrengh-
then my good defires, &
your charity, & compaf-
fion fill my fpirit with
holy meditations, to the
end that vaine thoughts
may find no place the-
rein.

Powre out the water of your grace, to quench the fyre of Concupiscence, that burneth in my heart; and gird my Reynes with the girdle of chastity, for otherwise I cannot be pleasing, nor acceptable vnto your selfe a Virgin so pure & holy.

5. Teach me (O Blessed Virgin) the way to subdue sinne, & to free my selfe from the flaming

ming furnace therof, in which I am scorched; for of my selfe I cannot returne to the right way, from whence I haue strayed.

I haue wept all the night, & my pillow hath bene bathed in my teares; but your hand hath soone taken me out of this sadnes, & I haue receiued consolation from you.

Be you euer Blessed

(O Queene of Heauen)
for it is your grace, that
doth assist me; & blessed
be sweet IESVS the fruit
of your wombe, for it is
he, who hath deliuered
vs from the bondage of
the diuell, and secured
vs from eternall death.

6. Blessed be the Name
of Mary, for it is that
Name alon which hath
bene found acceptable
before the face of God.
Let its Praise be euer

sunge

sunge by the mouths of Angells; and let afwell Heauen as Earth giue vnto it, the glory which it hath merited.

The great King of Kings hath chofen her for his mother becaufe of her Humility; and by her meanes peace hath bene brought into the world, & our aduerfary loft the aduátage which he had againft vs

She hath not onely

giuen vs her sonne, to redeeme vs , but also hath bene the cause that we haue the true Sacraments, which he hath left vnto his Church, in which the wyne is changed into his bloud, by whose meanes water was changed into wyne.

7. Teach me (O holy Virgin) to beleeue with you, that the works of your Sonne are aboue the course of Nature, of

which

which he is Author, and that I may not doubt, but that he who could change the firft, could alfo eafily change the fecond, by the vertue of his Word.

Lift vp thy felfe (O my foule) & infufe into thy heart the medita-tions of the miracles done by the interceffion of this holy Virgin; and put into my lips words to finge out her praifes,

F 4   that

that thou maiest find mercy with her, when thy Aduersaries drawe neere to assaile thee.

Thou canst suffer neither tribulation nor sorrow if thou retire thy selfe to this Virgin, for she will turne thé away from thee by her sweetnes; and they will seeke thee in vaine, to compasse thee about with misery, and calamity.

8. Let your right hand

hãd alwaies defend me,
(O Virgin euer ready to
ayde vs) & let mine ene-
mies be put to flight by
the strength of your
arme ; and all those who
hate you , fall downe at
your feet , that being
so chasticed they may
learne to humble them-
selues.

Susteyne the impe-
tuous assaults that they
make against me, and let
the workes that they

F 5   inuent

inuent to ouerwhelme
me, fall vpon their owne
heads : and let them say
themselues, We haue as-
saulted him in vaine, for
he is too well prouided
of succour.

9. Haue pitty on your
seruants (O B. Virgin)
haue pitty on thé, since
they call vpó your holy
Name; make hast to hel-
pe them, euen in the vio-
lence of the euill that
vrgeth them, and suffer

not

not the temptation, to
get victory ouer them.

Your holy Sonne hath
put in your right hand
the power to deliuer vs
from dangers ; wherfore
we implore hūbly your
ayd, and fuccour , afwell
in the vncertaine dan-
gers of the land , as the
fortunes and perills of
the fea.

He hath likewife put
vpon your head a Cro-
wne of fhininge Dia-

F 6   monds;

monds; for the miracles
which you haue done,
are the Trophyes of
your glory, & the Chur-
ches built throughout
the world in your ho-
nour, giue moſt ample
teſtimony therof.

10 Grant me a place
neere vnto you (O moſt
Glorious Virgin) that
when I haue paſſed the
bitter dolours, and trou-
bles of this life, I may
repoſe in the lap of your
sweet

sweet mercy, and compassion.

I will frequent your Altars in the Churches which are dedicated to you, & there will I exalt your sacred Name, since that of you is borne the sunne of Iustice, and the saluation of the world, and that they who trust in you, shall not be frustrate of their hope.

THE

THE HYMNE

Christus dum præsens.

CHrist when once present, & a
         guest,
   At a freindly nuptiall feast,
With all the rest that came, was set
   At table likewise for to eat.
To whom the Virgin Mother deare,
   Who likewise then was present
      there,
Sayd, with Charity all-deuine,
   These people, Sonne, haue lacke of
      wyne.
Whereat, the pots he bid to fill
   With water, which done to his will

By

By the pure vertue of his Word,
  Did most excellent wine affoord.
O wondrous power vnlimited,
  Who all hath made assoone as said !
Vpon this day you gaue a signe
  Of your Sacrament diuine.
Nor could it be a harder matter
  To you, who wyne did make of
    water,
With as much ease, in the same fashion
  To make another transmutation.
Water was wyne made at this feast,
  Whereat you were the chiefest
    guest:
Euen so, in th'Altars Sacrifice
  Wyne changed is to bloud likewise.
To you all glory be therefore
  I E S V S, that Blessed Mary bore:
To God the Father Lord of might,
  And to the holy Paraclite.

THE

THE SEAVENTH

PETITION.

Aue Maria gratia plena Dominus tecũ, benedicta tu in mulieribus, & benedictus fructus ventris tui IESVS. Sancta Maria mater Dei, ora pro nobis &c.

Mary, Mary, Mary,	
Mary, Mary, Mary,	
Mary, Mary, Mary,	Most Blessed Mary,
Mary, Mary, Mary,	constant
Mary, Mary, Mary,	at the
Mary, Mary, Mary,	foote of
Mary, Mary, Mary,	the Crosse, pray
Mary, Mary, Mary,	for me.
Mary, Mary, Mary,	
Mary, Mary, Mary,	

O

O BLESSED Virgin
Mary, who haue
borne with such con-
stancy so many dolours
and afflictions, on the
day of the Passion of
our Lord IESVS Christ
your sonne, grant that I
may be constant in all
my sorrowes and affli-
ctions.

I put the hope of my
saluation, in the confi-
dence which I haue, to
find compassion with
you;

you; and my soule moo-
ued with the afflictiõs of
this world, hath desire to
quench its thirst in the
dew of your grace, for it
seeketh after you, as the
Hart doth after the foũ-
taine of water, when he
is a thirst.

2. Let my sinnes be
washed, and cleansed in
the streames of your san
ctity, and let me be in-
cited to follow you, by
the integrity and purity

of

of your life, imitating
the perfections of your
sacred Vertues.

You are she who haue
allyed vs (although vn-
worthy sinners) in bro-
therhood with Christ
Iesvs; and can more
easily, if you please ,
ioyne vs to him by the
allyance of Loue , and
Charity.

3. Without you, we
had bene prisoners vn-
der the perpetuall sla-

uery

uery and tyranny of the
diuell : but you haue
freed vs from his vnsup-
portable yoke ; & from
a perpetuall exile , haue
brought vs to the King-
dome of the Bleſſed.

We haue bene made
companions, & fellow-
Cittizens with the An-
gells in Eternall Beati-
tude and all thoſe who
are dead , by inuocating
your holy Name, whilſt
they were aliue , haue

bene

bene receiued, and pla-
ced neere vnto you.

4. Grant then (O ho-
ly Virgin Mary indowed
with so exceedinge Cle-
mency) that I may ad-
dresse my prayers wholy
vnto you ; that so you
may present them to
your Sonne, who in fa-
uour of you will heare
me.

Looke vpon me (O
most sweet Virgin) look
vpon me with your eye

of

of pitty; and let the ho-
ly beames therof make
warme my foule, for you
are the light and guide
of thofe who haue put
their hope in you.

Drop downe vpõ me
the dew of that compaf-
fionate Affection which
fo shines in you; pur-
ginge my foule from
all the iniquities with
which it is defiled, and
for which it hath not
done due penance, and

satifsatisfaction.

5. I will confesse before you, against my selfe, the sinnes which I haue done, & giue testimony of the truth, when I do accuse my selfe of the wickednes which I haue comitted, that you may enioyne me heere my punishment, and I may make my Purgatory in this world.

For I hope that you will receyue me into

your

your protection, & giue
me conſtancy to beare
the afflictions which are
ſent me, in punishment
of my ſinnes; and that
I shall find the refre-
shment of your deuine
grace, in the middeſt of
my dolours.

6. The Heauens ſinge
forth your glory, the
Earth ſets out your pra-
iſe, and the Sea ſpreads
abroad the fame of your
miracles; wherſore you

are

are inuocated by all the whole Church of the Elect.

O all yee people, wher-soeuer disperfed, euen to the remoteft Regions of the world, reioyce at the prayfes of this holy Virgin ; and all together lift vp your voyces to Heauen in her honour.

She is the port of Saluation, & by her we enter into life in this world the heauens haue bene

G   made

made our inheritance,
since that from her is is-
sued the Word Eternall,
the only sonne of God.

7. This is that most
chast Virgin, who hath
bene a mother, and this
most chast Mother who
hath remained a Virgin
after her deliuery; and
this is she likewise, who
is the Creature, and mo-
ther of her Creatour.

The Penitent sinners
haue sayd, that you are

the

the hope, & the wicked
haue laughed them to
fcorne ; their laughinge
is fallen vpon them, for
Heauen (of which you
are the gate) hath bene
fhut againft thé, & Hell
hath fwallowed thé vp.

8. Keepe me from fo
great a danger (O Holy
Virgin, filled with all
bleffings) for I haue ab-
horred the abhomina-
ble wordes of thofe who
detract your holy name

I haue sayd to my selfe ; How longe will you be so patient , not to take notice of the iniuries that are done vnto you ? and require vengeance for them , at the handes of your deare sonne IESVS?

I remēber your Mercy, & Clemency, & haue thought , that if they would conuert themselues to you , that their sinnes should be forgotten,

ten, becaufe that you de-
fire not the death of a
finner, but rather that
he turne from his wic-
kednes, and liue, which
makes me alfo hope to
find grace with you: for
if you are fo fauourable
to thofe, who haue of-
feded you, when they ac-
knowledge their faults;
what will you be to
thofe, who haue called
vpon you, from their
Childhood?

9. O sacred Virgin, giue me grace to perseuere in offeringe my prayers vnto you, & put words in my mouth, which may be most pleasing vnto you.

Hearke graciously vnto me, that by the effects thereof I may know you to be neere vnto me; for enioying your holy grace & fauour, I can neuer defile my soule, in the foule ordure, and

filth

filth of sinne.

10. I will alwayes haue my soule cleane & pure, when I present my prayers vnto you, that you may be thereby pleased to heare me, and will acknowledge those benefits, which I haue receaued, to haue proceeded from your hands, & not from the hands of men, in whom there is no trust.

Be you alwaies Blef-

sed,

sed, (O queene of An-
gels) and be all they,
who praise your holy
Name, and exalt the ma-
gnificéce of your Great-
nes, blessed both by god,
and you, for euer and
euer .

THE

THE HYMNE

Stabat mater dolorosa.

THe mother *stood with griefes con-
      founded*,
   *Neere the Crosse, her teares
      abounded*,
   *While her deare sonne hanging
      was:*
*Through whose soule her sighes forth
      venting,*
   Sadly mourning, & lamenting,
   Sharpest points of swords did passe.
O how sad, and how distressed,
   Was that mother euer Blessed,
   Who Gods only sonne forth brought!

G 5   *She*

She in greife, and woes did languish,
　Quaking to behold, what anguish
　To her noble Sonne was wrought.
Who is he that teares could smother,
　If he saw our Saviours mother,
　In such bitter panges remaine!
Who could stint sad griefes assailing,
　To behold the mother wayling,
　For her Sonnes desertles paine!
For th'Offences of his Nation,
　She saw him in tribulation,
　And with cruell scourges rent.
Her sweet Sonnes departure seing,
　He in desolation being,
　When his last breath forth he sent,
Mother fountaine of true louing,
　Me to feele thy sorrow mouing
　Cause, that I may mourne with
　thee.
Let my hart with feruour burned,
　Towards Christ with loue be turned
　Which to him may pleasing be.

O

O most holy Mother hasten
   Firmely in my hart to fasten
   Strokes of him thus crucified.
Of thy Sonne with wounds tormented,
   Much t'endure for me contented,
   All the paines with me deuide.
Let my teares with thine be flowing,
   While I liue Compassion showing,
   With him on the Crosse opprest.
Neere the Crosse with thee remaining,
   To beare part of thy complaining,
   I most willingly request.
Made in fame all Maides excelling,
   Be not harsh my prayers repelling,
   But let me with thee complayne.
Let my mind Chrifts death still carry
   In my hart th'impression tarry,
   Of his Crosse, and bitter paine.
Let me with his strokes be wounded,
   With this Crosse my sense con-
      founded,
   For thy Sonnes beloued sake.

Thus inflam'd with hoat affection,
  Virgin, grant me thy protection,
  When all foules their iudgement
    take.
Let me with the Croffe be tended,
  With the death of Chrift defended,
  And ftill cherift with his grace.
When my body yields to dying,
  Let my foule to heauen flying,
  There obtaine a glorious place.

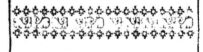

THE

THE EIGHT
PETITION.

Aue Maria gratia plena Dominus tecũ, benedicta tu in mulieribus, & benedictus fructus ventris tui I E S V S. Sancta Maria mater Dei, ora pro nobis &c.

Mary, Mary, Mary,
Mary, Mary, Mary,
Mary, Mary, Mary,
Mary, Mary, Mary,
Mary, Mary, Mary,
Mary, Mary, Mary,
Mary, Mary, Mary,
Mary, Mary, Mary,
Mary, Mary, Mary,
Mary, Mary, Mary,

Blessed Virgin Mary, whose hart vvas pierced vvith the ivvord of sorrovv, pray for me.

Q

O BLESSED Vir-
gin most excellent
in all Goodnes, & good
by all Excellency, I haue
seen the afflicted to haue
had recourse to you, &
they haue bene comfor-
ted; I beseech you giue
me the grace to call vpō
your holy ayd in my af-
flictions, to the end I
may feele the dew of
your Benignity, descen-
ding downe vpon me,
and receyue consolation
like

like vnto them.

My soule hath bene troubled with the dolours of this world, and I haue had none about me to succour me: my neighbours, and frends haue forsaken me, and haue laughed at the misfortunes which haue be fallen me.

2. I haue had recourse to your ayde, and haue found you ready to succour me, for asmuch as

you

you haue caſt your eyes
vpon me from the hi-
gheſt Heauens; & whilſt
my mouth hath byn fild
with your praiſes, my
heart hath felt refresh-
ment through the ho-
ny of your ſweetnes.

You are the fayre Cy-
preſſe, vnder the ſhad-
dow of which I repoſe
my ſelfe, oppreſſed with
vehement heat of the
tentations of this world;
and it is you who haue
quen-

quenched my insupportable thirst with the water of the profound well of your Consolation.

3. Come vnto her all yee that are thirsty, and she will giue you willingly to drinke; and when you haue once tasted of her waters, you will presently come vnto her, for that no Aromaticall drinkes, are so sweet and delicious as they.

Pray vnto her that

with

with this same water, she
will wash away the fil-
thines of your sinnes,
and so your soule may
shine in purity; that be-
inge made cleane from
all vices, it may appeare
without spot, before the
face of her Sonne Christ
IESVS.

4. Let my hart lan-
guish (O Blessed Vir-
gin) in your loue, & be
wounded with your fa-
uours, that it may be

made

made capable to receyue your benefits, & worthy to enioy with you, for euer, the celestiall Beatitude of the Kingdome of the Blessed.

I will seeke with all my power the increase of your Glory, and I will present vnto you euery day the incense of my poore prayers; and in all Congregations and Solemnities, I will blesse your Name, makinge

knowne,

knowne how great it is,
& how much reueréced
throughout the whole
world.

5. I will giue you the
Honour which is due
vnto you, seing that God
himselfe hath vouchsa-
fed so much to honour
you, as to choose you to
be the Mother of his
onely Sonne; & the An-
gels haue bowed their
knees before you in all
Humility.

Bal-

Ballance this Honour
with that sorrow which
seized vpon your sacred
hart so bitterly, whē you
held your most beloued
and Blessed Sonne bet-
wixt your armes, after he
was taken downe from
the Crosse, wheron the
Iewes had cruelly, and
ignominiously crucified
him.

6. Direct me (O most
holy Virgin, how I shall
behaue my selfe towards

you;

you ; for what can I, (Wretched Sinner) do worthy of your merits ; to whō the greatest Powers, & Dominations are subiect!

Supply in me that which may be wanting, & excuse my infirmity, because in the presence of your Maiesty, I shall be found most abiect, if I be not assisted with your good fauour, and that your hand be not

fauou-

fauourably stretched out to lift me vp.

Who is like vnto you, eyther in grace or glory and vnto whom haue the Heauens serued as a footstoole, but to you? The Kings of the Earth are great, and their Maiesty is feared amonge men, but to you the Angels, & all the creatures which are in heauen, do obey.

7. You are that daugh-ter

ter of Sion, who are the spouse of the liuinge God, and mother of his Sonne Christ IESVS, and who do raigne most happily among the Blessed in Paradise; for there is no contention or strife, nor any to call your Kingdome & Souerainty in question.

I will praise your Greatnes for euer, and will alwaies place your miracles before mine eyes,

because

becaufe you will be my
fafeguard and protectiõ,
and deliuer me from the
hands of mine enimyes.

I will put my truft in
you, and thereby shall
not hope in vaine; be-
caufe thofe who confide
in your mercy, shall re-
ceyue a crowne of the
beames of your Grace;
& the heauens will fall
vnto them for their in-
heritance.

8. Incyte my fpirit (O

H   Bleffed

Blessed Virgin) to loue
your goodnes , and let
my soule magnify you,
for your benefits are
great towards me ; and I
haue receiued of your
bounty, more then I can
euer deserue.

You haue preserued
me both by day and
night, & haue giuen me
in charge to my Angell
Guardian , that he haue
speciall care of me ; and
at my rising out of my
bed,

bed, I haue giuen you thanks, for without you I should fall into a thou-sand dangers.

Keep me euer, in like manner, from all euill, and let me know more and more that you aſſiſt me, to the end, that I may likewiſe more and more increaſe in loue to-wards you, leaſt I be-come vnthankefull for all the benefits which you beſtow vpon me.

9. If I haue at any time indured affliction, and mine enemies haue triū-phed ouer me, it hath bene becaufe of my fin-nes; but now if they come vnto me, I will haue recourfe to you, becaufe you will do me the fauour to preuent all fuch euill, and I will call vpon you before that it happen vnto me.

Turne away I hum-

bly

bly befeech you, by your
vertue and power, the
euill tentations, which
inuiron my heart, that
they may not hinder me
to worke my faluation;
for if I fall into finne, the
punishment will follow
me: & if I refift the fame,
you will caufe me to be
rewarded in Heauen.

Let my praiers come
euer vnto the eares of
your Compaffion, and
let them mooue you to

H 3 heare

heare me; & my mouth
shall shew forth your
Clemécy to strange Na-
tions, & they shall con-
fesse vnto you, in sin-
ging forth your glory.

10. Heale my woun-
ded heart with the sweet
oyntment of your pie-
ty, for you are she who
haue healed the almost-
incurable wound, which
our first Father had ma-
de in humane Nature;
& haue brought againe

to

to life all those who were in the way of death and perdition.

Those who hope in you (O most holy Virgin) shall find the treasures of peace, after that they are departed out of this world: & those who inuocate the holy Name of Mary , shall arriue, together with the Blessed, to eternall beatitude; for the kingdome of Heauen is full of those, of whom you haue had pitty, and compaſſion.

I will therefore ſing Hymnes and praiſes in your honour, and will bleſſe you, to the end, that when my ſoule departeth from this body, you may make it repoſe in the grace of IESVS CHRIST.

THE

THE HYMNE
Fortè dum vides.

O How extreme the dolour was,
   The which vpon your hart did
  gnaw ;
Mother most sweet & full of grace,
   When as our Sauiour dead you
  saw:
I thinke no weapon could be found,
   How sharpe or keene so ere it
  were,
The which could giue so great a wound,
   Vnto your heart, as it had there.
Into a deadly sound you fell,
   When as your Sonne you there did
  see,

By

By thoſe fierce Miniſters of Hell,
  Brought vnto ſuch extremity.
Yet ſo intollerable was,
  His ſcorners iniuries ſo ſore,
That e'uen the launce his hart did paſſe
  Could ſcarſe afflict or grieue you
    more.
O holy Virgin, Grant I may
  His torments, & his cruell blowes
So feele within my ſoule alway,
  To worke ſaluation out of thoſe.
And let me haue the thornes, the launce,
  The rods, the nayles, and holy
    Croſſe,
For euer in my remembrance,
  With you for to bewaile his loſſe.
All glory euer be to you
  Sweet IESVS, Bleſſed Maryes
    ſonne;
The like vnto the Father too,
  And holy Ghoſt, whilſt ages runne.

THE

THE NINTH
PETITION.

Aue Maria gratia plena Dominus
tecū, benedicta tu in mulieribus,
& benedictus fructus ventris tui
IESVS. Sancta Maria mater Dei,
ora pro nobis &c.

Mary, Mary, Mary,
Mary, Mary, Mary,
Mary, Mary, Mary,
Mary, Mary, Mary,
Mary, Mary, Mary,
Mary, Mary, Mary,
Mary, Mary, Mary,
Mary, Mary, Mary,
Mary, Mary, Mary,
Mary, Mary, Mary,

Most Blessed Virgin Mary, Queene of Angels, pray for me.

O HOLY Virgin Mary, who are accustomed to shew your selfe, as ready to succour, as the afflicted are to call vpon you; grant me grace to perseuere in those vertues which are most pleasing vnto you, and principally in that which hath caused God to loue you, and to chuse you among all women, to be the mother of his deare and onely Sonne.

Bring

Bring downe the pry-
de of my heart, & make
it so humble, that it may
abase it selfe euen before
the poorest Creature of
the earth, for they are
members of God; and he
might if he had pleased,
haue made me more
poore & miserable then
any of them all.

2. The Prophet *Esay*
hath sayd, The valleys
should be raised into
moūtaines, & the moun-

taines

taines should become as
the valleys; by which he
hath giuen vs to vnder-
stand, that the haughty
and proude should be
humbled, but the hum-
ble and obedient should
be exalted: so in like mā-
ner, because you made
your selfe little in the
eies of men, & would be
called onely the Hum-
ble Hand-maid of our
Lord, he therefore was
pleased that Christ Iesus

the

the eternall Word shold take humane fleshe in your sacred wombe.

Gird my Reynes with the girdle of Chastity, and let the fire of Concupiscence be quite extinguished in me, by the sweet dew of your grace: for an vnchast heart cannot be pleasing to you who haue so pure a soule.

3. Let me by your exáple learne to be patient in my aduersities, since

you

you haue borne such an infinite number of afflictions so patiently, in the time of the most dolorous passion of your dearest Sonne IESVS our Sauiour, and Redeemer.

Make me to imploy my selfe in holy workes, like vnto those three holy Maryes, who went to visit the sacred body of your Sonne in the Sepulcher, and let me with

you

you beleiue his words af-
furedly; for you doubted
not , but that he was to
rife the third day, according as he had promi-
fed.

4. Be pleafed to take
from my hart (O moft
charitable Virgin) all
hatred, rancour, and en-
mity againft my neigh-
bour-, for you haue bene
gracious to all ; neyther
hath Enuy euer made
you fpeake ill of any, no

not

not so much of those cruell enemyes, who so inhumanely crucifyed your sweet IESVS.

Grant also that I may passe my life in imitation of yours, as neere as it may be possible, to the end that giuing my selfe to those things that may be pleasing to you, I may likewise please you, and so be receiued with you into the celestiall Beatitude, for euer.

5. The

5. The Angels reioyce
when your holy workes
are imitated, and your
actions published by vs,
for they are Admirable
in the eies of men, and
moſt Holy before the
face of God, who from
the wombe of your mo-
ther hath choſen you to
be the mother of his
onely Sonne.

He shall do a thing
much pleaſing both to
ſweet Iesvs, & to your

selfe

selfe, who shall imitate any action of yours; for you haue pleased him in all things, & he hath not found any thing to re-prehēd in all that which you haue done.

We are infinitely bo-und to imitate your ver-tues, for therby we haue purchased vnto our sel-ues a great allyance, and we haue bene made the children of God, & co-heyres of the kingdome

of

of Heauen.

6. Man hath by your meanes bene seated at the right hand of God, and you haue bene lifted vp to his throne of glory: Wherfore I will adore prostrate before you, and with teares in mine eyes will I confesse vnto you all the sinnes, that I haue euer committed.

Obtaine for me I hūbly beseech you, of your deare Sonne I E S V s, full

remis-

remiſſion of my ſinnes, and when I ſhall come before him to be iudged, take you in hand the defence of my cauſe, and become my Aduocate, becauſe I haue no other to whom I may ſafely fly, or retire my ſelfe.

7. Riſe vp, O all yee Creatures of God, and come with me to render prayſe & thankes to this moſte Worthy Virgin; ſinge vnto her ſonges of

joy,

ioy, in magnifying her glory, and exalting the sacred Name of Mary.

You Patriarches and Prophets sing her praises to the Heauens; and you Apostles and Martyrs of Iesvs Christ, ioyne your voyces with the, & all together with sweet harmony exalt her merits.

And all yee holy Confessors, who haue defended the faith which she

did

did hold; and all yee sa-
cred Virgins, who haue
followed her pure Cha
ſtity, and became the
ſpouſes of her Bleſſed
Sonne, lift vp your ſweet
voyces in her honour,
and make the Heauens
ſound with her Hymnes
and prayſes.

8. The Angels, Ar-
changels, Cherubims,
Seraphims, Thrones, &
Dominations haue byn
the firſt, who haue exal

ted

ted her, and to the sound of Organs, Lutes, and other melodious instruments haue sunge forth the Hymnes of her prayses and merits.

All the Inhabitants and Cittizés of Paradise haue gloryfied her, and the very Heauens, the Ayre, the Earth and the Sea haue adored her, as their soueraigne Queen. for her power is exten ded ouer them; because

I   God

God hath made her Queene ouer all his kingdome.

O most holy Virgin, how admirable is your name throughout all the world ! Grant me Grace to acknowledge the greatnes which is in you, and then I shall honour you according to your merits.

9. He that shall haue the Character of this name of *Mary* ingrauen

in

in his heart, shall be
regiſtred in the booke
of life: his enimyes shall
want power to hurt him
& he shall at laſt enioy
the life eternall.

I will haue this Name
alwayes in my mouth,
wherfore she will ſtretch
forth the shield of her
right Arme, to beare of
the blowes of my aduer-
ſaryes, and will aſſiſt me
by her power; and so I
shall be freed from the

pe-

perills and dangers in-
cident to this miserable
life.

Teach me the way of
Equity, that I may fur-
ther imitate this vertue
of yours : for he who
doth Iustice to others,
shall find Iustice him-
selfe; & whosoeuer doth
iniustice, his sinnes shall
fall vpon him, and euill
shall not go from his
house.

10. My heart hath de-
sired

fired to be pleasing to
Christ IESVS, and my
soule hath sayd vnto it
selfe: Serue his holy Mo-
ther the Virgin Mary,
with all deuotion ; for
without doubt it will be
most pleasing to him,
since he himselfe hath
byn so obedient and ser-
uiceable vnto her.

Helpe me then, O
Blessed Virgin, to serue
you, and make me to
call vpon your Holy

I 3   Name

Name from the mor-
ning ; and awaking at
midnight , to confeſſe
my ſelfe vnto you , that
I may not ſleepe in ſinne
for feare leaſt death at
an inſtant deſtroy , and
kill both my body , and
ſoule .

THE

THE HYMNE
O Gloriosa Domina.

O *Glorious Lady Queene of might,*
Seated aboue the starry light;
Whose heauenly wisedome thee did
make ,
From sacred brest doth suste-
nance take ,
What wofull Eue had loß before ,
By beauteous branch thou doeß
restore :
That mourning wights 'mongß stars
might raigne ,
Tho'art made the entrance Hea-
uen to gaine.

I 4   *Thou*

Thou glorious gate of highest King,
   Thou Orient port whence light
      doth spring;
True light being brought by Virgins
      choyce,
   Redeemed Nations now reioyce.
Lord may thy glory still endure,
   Who borne wast of a Virgin pure,
The Fathers, & the Spirits of loue,
   Which endles worlds may not re-
      moue.

THE

THE TENTH
PETITION.

Aue Maria gratia plena Dominus
tecū, benedicta tu in mulieribus,
& benedictus fructus ventris tui
I E S V S. Sancta Maria mater Dei,
ora pro nobis &c.

Mary,	Mary,	Mary,	
Mary,	Mary,	Mary,	
Mary,	Mary,	Mary,	
Mary,	Mary,	Mary,	Blessed Virgin Mary, Queene of Prophets, pray for me.
Mary,	Mary,	Mary,	
Mary,	Mary,	Mary,	
Mary,	Mary,	Mary,	
Mary,	Mary,	Mary,	
Mary,	Mary,	Mary,	
Mary,	Mary,	Mary,	

I 5 O

O MOST holy Virgin Mary, which life hath bene so exemplar and commendable, that the Angels haue admired the same; giue me grace to confirme mine vnto yours, as farre as possibly I can, that I may thereby be more pleasing and acceptable to your Blessed Sonne Christ IESVS.

His life hath bene like vnto yours, and yours

like

like vnto his, both chaſt, both humble, both fauourable, both pittyfull both patient, and both indewed with a ſingular loue, towards humaine kind.

2. Extinguiſh the fire of Concupiſcence in my reynes, that I may conſerue my chaſtity, for that is the vertue which maketh our ſoule white, and inueſteth it with a faire linnen Stole, when

it

it is separated from the body .

Make me humble to euery one, for I haue no occasion to be proud, being but the slime of the earth , and a bubble of water filled with aire, which vanisheth away in a moment, and is turned to nothing.

Make me gentle towards all , because the cruell and wicked do giue ill example; and if

all

all the reſt ſhould doe the like, one might with more ſafety lead his life amonge wilde beaſtes, then men.

3. Make me pittifull towards the poore, and to haue compaſſion of their miſeries, for they are members of God, & ſhall poſſeſſe the goods of heauen, ſince that the goods of earth haue not giuen them occaſion to ſinne ; and in lieu of

the

the hunger which they haue endured, they shall be refreshed with celestiall graces.

Arme me with Patience against all Afflictions, for that is the way to ouercome them, since that our humaine conditiō permits vs not to be exempted from them; & that your Blessed Sonne himselfe and you also, haue tasted the bitternes thereof

4. Com

4. Comfort me, O most fauourable Virgin, like as your deare Sonne did comfort you, after his most dolourous passion, in appearing vnto you, to giue you to vnderstand that he was risen from death, and that the Prophesyes were then ended, and fully accomplished in him.

Incyte my heart to loue my neighbour, as my selfe, and let me

not

not detract from his good name, nor desire his goods, nor any thing which is his.

Kill within me the passions of Choller, and desire of Reuenge, for that your selfe had none against the barbarous & cruell Iewes, who without any feeling of humanity, so iniustly nailed your deare sonne, & my sweet Sauiour vnto the Crosse.

5. Stirre

5. Stirre vp my slouth with the zeale of your loue, and let myne eyes be opened by your grace, that I may see and acknowledge the loathsomnes of my sinnes; & let me haue horrour to fall againe into them, after that once by your gratious fauour I haue bene deliuered from them .

Direct my feet in the right pathes of your life,

for

for that is the right way which leads to heauen, and thofe who follow it, shall not wander from the life eternall , but ariue ynto the habitation and aboad of the Bleffed.

I will feparate my felfe far from the tumult of the world , that in my folitude I may be vifited by my Sauiour; for he doth not vfe to comfort any one , but

when

when he is quiet, and in contemplation of the mysteries of his blessed life.

6. Imploy my hands in those works in which yours were exercised, & blesse my labours, as yours haue beene Blessed; to the end that so my soule may be at rest, & I may haue sufficient to sustaine my selfe and family.

You forsake not those

who

who call vpon you : and
in making knowne our
neceſſityes to your Bleſ-
ſed Sonne, he ſuſtaineth
vs in time of famine; for
he it is , who feeds the
young Rauens whileſt
they are left, & forſaken
of their Dammes.

He nouriſheth thou-
ſands of people, making
bread to multiply in
their hands; he makes
the *Manna* to rayne from
Heauen ; & with a hard

flint

flint makes a fountaine to spring vp in the defart.

Euen then when we seeme to haue lost all hope, doth he graciously assist vs; & those things, which compared to our forces we haue thought impossible, he hath pleased to make easy vnto vs.

7. Pray for vs vnto him (O most Blessed Virgin) for he will giue eare vnto you; and your

sweet

sweet regard ioyned with the authority of a Mother, will turne his Iustice into Mercy; and so our Offences shall be wiped out of the booke of Accompt of our life.

Be you our Mediatresse, for we dare not be so bould as to haue recourse to him; and he would that you should be knowne to haue all authority both in Heauen and Earth, to be the

Soue-

Soueraigne Queene in his Celestiall Court, and Kingdome.

Let your Name and Memory be in the middest of my heart, & the Holynes of your life alwayes before mine eyes, that it may direct my actions according to the modell of yours; and therby vouchsafe to giue me the grace to perseuere in good, and to decline from all euill.

8. O

8. O Blessed Virgin, whose merits exceed all the praises of men, do not permit the wicked to blaspheme your holy Name, but let their tongue who speake euill of you, perish in their mouth.

The wicked haue opened their throates, and I haue heard words proceed from thence, more stinking then Carrion; they are more infected

then

then old graues or Se-
pulchers; for the ayre of
them is corrupt, and pe-
ftilence is entred amõg
them which hath made
defert and waft their fa-
milyes.

They haue feen their
children carryed to the
graue, they haue wept
ouer the Sepulchers of
their wyues; mortality
hath made their flocks
defolate, & their groũds
haue not rendered the

K   third

third part of that which was sowen.

9. Some of them haue acknowledged their sinnes and offences; and Plenty hath reuisited their houses; but those who haue remayned obstinate, haue dyed in their sinne, and become a prey vnto Hell, since heauen hath bene shut against them for euer.

I haue bene comforted to see my selfe out

of

of their company, & in safety from their pernicious designes, for they haue wished me euill, because I was iealous of your Honour.

They did bend theyr bowes against my fame and renowne, and you haue burst their strings, and broken their arrowes; and they haue gone about in vaine to hurt me, for I did place all my hope in you.

10. My

10. My life seemed reproachfull vnto them, because I laboured to conforme it vnto yours; they found fault with all my actions, and in euery place where they met together, they laughed at me.

You haue confounded them, and I haue bene safe ; malediction hath dwelt in their houses ; & your blessing hath not departed from myne :

Peace

Peace hath inhabitated with me, and the dew of your grace hath flowed in my foule, and I haue receyued it into my heart.

I will euer bleſſe you, and exalt your Holy Name, becauſe your benefits are great towards me, & I expect yet a greater reward in heauen in the company of the Bleſſed Soules.

THE

THE HYMNE
Consolator optime.

O Most gracious Comforter,
  Who when the Pascha ended,
To your Mother did appeare,
  From Lymbo new ascended.
Whome alone you found shut vp
  In deepest meditation
Of that most sad and bitter cup
  You dranke off in your Passion.
Who can thinke to how much ioy
  Of heart it did restore you;
When sodainly you lookt, and saw
  Our Sauiour there before you?

As

As great as was your greife before
   To see his paine and anguish;
Euen with as great a ioy, or more,
   He made you now to languish.
Grant euen so, O Mother sweete,
   Our life heere being passed,
That we in Heauen that light may
      meete
   And with it be imbraced.
To you all honour, Lord of Host,
   This Blessed Maryes Sonne;
To the Father, and Holy Ghost,
   Whilst Times, and Ages run.

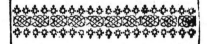

THE ELEAVENTH
PETITION

Aue Maria gratia plena Dominus tecū, benedicta tu in mulieribus, & benedictus fructus ventris tui IESVS. Sancta Maria mater Dei, ora pro nobis *&c.*

Mary, Mary, Mary,	
Mary, Mary, Mary,	
Mary, Mary, Mary,	
Mary, Mary, Mary,	Most Blef-
Mary, Mary, Mary,	fed Mary,
Mary, Mary. Mary,	Queene
Mary, Mary, Mary,	of Virgins
Mary, Mary, Mary,	pray for
Mary; Mary, Mary,	me.
Mary, Mary, Mary,	
Mary, Mary, Mary,	

I

I Most humbly beseech you, O Virgin most admirable in all your works, to giue me grace, to put all my hope in you, whē my soule is troubled with tribulation, for I knowe that I shall not be fruſtrated, becauſe that your mercy is greater then I can poſſibly conceiue in my mind.

All thoſe who haue truſted in you, haue had

K 5   cauſe

cause to blesse & prayse you; for that which they haue desired hath befallen them, and ioy hath entred into theyr soules, before any Affliction could oppresse them.

2. O my Soule, hope then in this Blessed Virgin, for asmuch as I will confesse my selfe againe vnto her, and her pittifull eyes shall be turned towrds me: Her right Hand shall saue me frō

the

the troubles which euen
drowne me in the bit-
ternes of their waters.

The waues of tribula-
tion haue beaten againſt
the ship, wherein I ſay-
led ouer the miſeryes of
this world, and haue al-
moſt ſwallowed me vp
into their depthes; but
you (O Bleſſed Virgin)
ready to help, haue ſa-
ued me from their dan-
gers, and by your ayd I
am ariued at the port of

ſafety,

safety, & consolation.

I haue seene the perills & dangers which hange ouer our heads in this life, and their accidents are very fearfull, and terrible ; Preserue me by your pittifull Goodnes , and let my soule often remember them , that thereby it may not be puffed vp with the wind & breath of Pryde.

Your Grace and Clemency

mency haue drawne me
to you, and haue ftirred
me vp to loue you with
all affection; fuffer me
not, I befeech you, to
haue hoped in vaine, for
the mercy which you
shew to them who call
vpon you, doth redoūd
to the glory of your ho-
ly Name.

Giue the reward of
victory to thofe who
haue put their truft in
you, and let them euer

bleffe

blesse and praise your mercy, participating of your benefits in this world, and of the recompence which you will bestow vpon them, in the next.

4. The rich Foole hath trusted in his great wealth and riches, but Barrennes hath come, and he hath bene hungry, and theeues haue broken into his house, & borne away his trea-

sure:

sure:the fall of his proud
Buildings hath ouer
whelmed him, and his
Children haue begged
their food.

I haue said to my selfe,
See how he hath put his
trust in his goods! I will
not imitate him, but will
hope in the Blessed Vir-
gin, and she will take
me, togeather with all
my family into her pro-
tection and safeguard.

5. No one hayre of

my head shall fall without her permiſſion, for she hath nūbred them, and the leaſt part of my goods shall not perish, becauſe I haue put them into her hands; & I will preſent vpon her Altar, the tenth Part of all which I poſſeſſe.

She will reſtore a hundred fould of all which is giuen vnto her, & for a little thing preſented in her honour,

she

she giues eternall lyfe;
and opens the treasures
of her liberality in the
glory of Paradise.

Her friendship is of
more worth then all the
riches of the world, and
her grace is more to be
esteemed, then gold and
pretious stones; for we
shall carry nothing of
them away when we de-
part; but they who par-
take of her graces shall
be sure of them for euer.

6.

6 I will prayse you (O admirable Virgin) and magnify your holy Name, in the increase of those graces : Put into my mouth words which may expresse them, and which may be pleasing vnto you .

You are the Queene of Heauen, the Lady of the Angels, the Spouse of the liuing God, Mother of his onely Sonne, Protectresse of the poore

and

and orphans, the stay of Wydowes, the Aduocate of sinners, the Glory of Virgins, and Comfortresse of the afflicted.

7. You are the beloued of the Holy Ghost, the Vessell of Election, the Rod of Iesse, the tree of life, the Starre of the sea, the Mirrour of Iustice, the Throne of wisedome, the Tower of Dauid, and the Fountaine of all sweetnes.

You

You are the Princesse of the Apostles, the Mistresse of the Prophets, the light of the Euangelists, the Glory of Martyrs, the truth of Confessors, the Praise of the Innocents, the Gate of Paradise, the Treasure of Holynes, the Fountaine of mercy, the example of humility, & Sanctuary of the Incarnate Word.

8. You are the Rose

without

without prickles, the
fruitfull Palme, the im-
mortall Lawrell, the
Terrestriall Paradise,
the Garden of pleasure,
the Celestiall Manna,
the Citty of God, the
odoriferous Cypresse,
the sauoury Plant, the
Port of health, and the
Sanctuary of all Secu-
rity.

You are she who first
(after our Sauiour Iesus
Christ) haue carryed

our

cur Humanity into hea-
uen ; for euen as in your
fight he afcended to re-
fume his place at the
right hand of God his
Father, fo he hath affum-
pted you from among
mortall men, that your
facred body, frō whence
he had taken his owne,
might be preferued free
from all corruption.

9. Bleffed be he who
ceafeth not to praife
you (O moft excellent
Virgin)

Virgin;) and be he like-
wise happy who taketh
delight, to heare your
Vertues spoken of, and
your Excellencies re-
counted.

I will make comme-
moration off your Mer-
uailes, and my soule
shall be rauished with
your Greatnes, that I
may with more honour,
and reuerence, adore
your Maiesty, acknow-
ledging before you, how

vn-

vnworthy and abiect I
am to befeech you to do
any thing in my fauour.

10. It will be pleafing
vnto you, that I humble
my felfe by prayer be-
fore you, for you giue
eare vnto the humble,
but the proude do find
your eares deafe vnto
their prayers.

Turne your face to-
wards me, & regard me
with the eye of your
mercy, otherwife I fhall

be

be in doubt of my salua-
tion, since that I haue alwaies put my hope in
you, & haue bine confi-
dent that you would not
leaue me in necessity.

Your spirit is without
guile, & you neuer fru-
strate the desire of those
who call vpon you : Be
mindfull of me, & haue
more regard to my will
which hath bene good,
then to the multitude
of my offences.

L   THE

THE HYMNE

Memento salutis Author.

Saluations Authour mindfull be,
  That once our forme so pleased thee,
That of pure Maid, our body ta'ne,
  To be new borne thou didest
    sustaine.
Mary the Mother of Heauens grace,
  Mother where-Mercy hath cheife
    place;
From cruell Foe our soules defend,
  And them receiue whē life shall end.
Lord may thy Glory still endure,
  Who borne wast of a Virgin pure:
The Father, and the spirits of loue,
  Which endles worlds may not re-
    moue.

                              THE

THE TVELVTH
PETITION.

Aue Maria gratia plena Dominus
tecũ, benedicta tu in mulieribus,
& benedictus fructus ventris tui
I E S V S. Sancta Maria mater Dei,
ora pro nobis &c.

Mary, Mary, Mary, ⎤
Mary, Mary, Mary, ⎥
Mary, Mary, Mary, ⎥
Mary, Mary, Mary, ⎥ BlessedVir-
Mary, Mary, Mary, ⎥ gin Mary,
Mary, Mary, Mary, ⎬ Queene of
Mary, Mary, Mary, ⎥ all Saints
Mary, Mary, Mary, ⎥ pray for
Mary, Mary, Mary, ⎥ me.
Mary, Mary, Mary, ⎦

EXCITE my soule to loue you (O glorious Virgin) who haue beene so cherished by God , that he would choose you from the wombe of your mother, to beare in your bowels, his onely Sonne ; and hath loued you more then all women, and honoured you more then all creatures besides .

He hath moreouer giuen you the assistance

of

of his holy Spirit in al your actions, whom he hath visibly sent vnto you vpō the day of Penticost, when you were in Company of the rest of the faithfull Apostles, to comfort you in his absence, vntill he might exalt you aboue all the Heauens, into the glory of his Paradise.

2. O let your loue descend into my heart from that place so high

and glorious; and let me desire nothing els, but to please you, in directing all my actions, according to the intention of your holy will.

Your beauty surpasseth all the Beautyes which are created; the Sunne and Moone giue way vnto you; the Angels themselues admire you, and the Heauens bend vnder your feet; wherefore I will loue no

other

other but you.

3. Let me see (O most Charitable Virgin) that face so singularly fayre, let me be so much inflamed with the loue of you, that I may neuer depart from out of your sight.

I will open the doore of my mouth vnto my heart, and it shall come forth to search after you; for it loues you, and you will receiue it, through

your singular goodnes,
into the bosome of that
loue, which so Seraphi-
cally inflamed you.

My lipps shall giue
way vnto my voyce, and
my tongue shall singe
forth your praise, be-
cause my soule is raui-
shed in Extasy with me-
ditating of your won-
drous beauty.

4. I will inflame my
affection towards you,
and will imitate your

Humi-

Humility, for that is the chiefeſt Vertue which hath ſo indecred you in the loue of God, and which hath made his Bleſſed Sonne to humble himſelfe, euen vnto earth, to take humaine fleſh of you.

Grant me the grace to be obedient to your commaundements, like as you haue bene obedient to the voyce of the Angell, when he

L 5 announ-

announced vnto you from God, that the euer lasting Word should be borne of you.

I haue desired to follow the footesteps of your chaste Virginity; dry vp in me I beseech you the waters of Concupiscence which seeke to drowne my heart; for their waues are more dangerous, then those of the sea, stirred vp by tempest.

5. Let

5. Let my eyes be clo-
sed vp in the shaddow
of this Transitory and
vayne world, that I may
behould more clearly
the glorious beames of
the Celestiall ; and let
them be alwaies lifted
vp on high, that all ear-
thly things may be vn-
knowne vnto them.

Keep my feet from
stumbling into sinne, &
let not the thoughts of
this world make me fall

L 6   to

to the earth, whilst I
haue mine eyes fixed
vpon you, but direct my
prayers to more cele-
ftiall Cogitations.

Make me partaker of
those riches, which you
inioy in heauen, when I
shall ariue vnto you; &
grant, that during the
pilgrimage of this life, I
may haue part of the fa-
uour of your graces.

6. The wicked shall
be conuerted vnto you;

seing

seing me assisted by you,
and say in their harts;
the power of her whom
he adores is great,& her
mercy is infinite,for she
aydeth him in all his
actions , and the workes
of his hands are full of
her benediction .

Let vs returne to this
Virgin , & she will haue
also pitty of vs , aswell as
of other sinners , who
haue implored her ayd,
and haue foūd her more

ready

ready to succour, then euer they durst hope for.

Let vs draw our selues out of the filthines wherin we haue so longe time slept, being euen drunken with our vices; and she will wash away, and cleanse all our iniquityes; since that she is most mercifull.

7. I will reioyce at the Conuersion of sinners, and the Angels shall

shall glorify you therefore; for from you proceedeth the very life of their Saluation, and your benefits are spread abroad euen vnto thousands.

Be as the Loadstone, O Blessed Virgin, to draw vnto you, the heauy Iron of my soule, that it may cleaue fast vnto you, and tast the fruites of the celestiall Beatitude, to inioy them

after.

afterward in a more perfect manner.

Let the Cords of your Mercy fasten me vnto you, and let the knot be kint theron for euer; for neare vnto your Tabernacle I shall be free frō the Ambushes of my enemyes, and shall inioy the Beatitude eternall.

8. You are the heyght of all solace and delectation, and by the dew of
your

your grace, you refresh the Soules oppressed with affliction, & make thē declare the miseryes with which they haue bene compassed about

The Ire of God is turned away from vs by you, and insteed of iudging vs according to his Iustice, he will iudge vs according to his Mercy; for your intercession is of wonderfully efficacy with him.

Those

Thoſe who loue you are beloued of him, and he loueth thoſe who are deare vnto you, wherefore I will place my affection on you, that I may vpon all occaſions find him propitious and fauourable vnto me.

9. Giue me grace (O moſt Meeke Virgin) to perſiſt in the deuotion wᶜʰ I haue vowed vnto you, enkindling in my hearte the fire of your

cele·

celeſtiall loue; and let me when I faile in my ſelfe, find my force and ſtrength in you.

Attend to the ſupplications, which I make vnto you, and haue regard to my humble deſires, & not to the ſmall number of good works, which I haue done, for my Enemyes do often hinder me from the effect, but they cannot alter my affection from

being

being right and good.

10. I haue not ceased
to cry vnto you all the
night, and you heard my
plaints, and I haue pre-
sently found, that you
haue succoured me, be-
cause my heart hath lea-
ped for ioy, euen whilst
I was drying vp the tea-
res from my eyes.

It is your hand which
hath touched me, and
which hath laboured in
my cause, when mine

ene-

enemyes did hold me beseiged; for I knew well that mine owne forces were too weake, to resist the violent assault of mine aduersaryes.

Breake (O my soule) breake the bonds of thy yoke, and leaue present-ly this body, in which thou art imprisoned, & go to enioy the eternall Beatitude, among those whom thou louest, and esteemest so deare.

THE

THE HYMNE
Beata nobis gaudia.

THe Sunnes returne from yearly
round,
Makes all our harts with ioy
abound:
When as the holy Spirits light,
Did shine vpon th' Apostles bright.
And with a cleere and trembling flame,
Of fiery tongues in likenes came:
That both their Eloquence might flow,
And Charity more ardent grow.
Ech tongue they vnderstood and spake,
Which did the Gentils wōder make,

VVho

Who iudged them with wyne opprest,
  Whome so the holy Ghost had blest.
All this by Mystery was done,
  The Pascha being past and gone,
That sacred time, in which committed
  Sinnes, by the law were all remit-
    ted.
Our breasts vnto thee long since vowed,
  With thy grace thou hast in-
    dowed ;
Forgiue vs all our sinfull crymes,
  And giue vnto vs peacefull times.
All Glory vnto God in Heauen,
  And to the holy Ghost be giuen:
Vnto the Sonne, whom Mary bore
  From hence forth now, and euer-
    more.

THE

THE THIRTEENTH
PETITION.

Aue Maria gratia plena Dominus
tecū, benedicta tu in mulieribus,
& benedictus fructus ventris tui
IESVS. Sancta Maria mater Dei,
ora pro nobis &c.

Mary, Mary, Mary,
Mary, Mary, Mary,
Mary, Mary, Mary,
Mary, Mary, Mary,
Mary, Mary, Mary,
Mary, Mary, Mary,
Mary, Mary, Mary,
Mary, Mary, Mary,
Mary, Mary, Mary,
Mary, Mary, Mary,

Most Blessed Mary, grant me to thinke duly on my death

O

O Most sweet Virgin mother of Christ IESVS, Mistresse & companion of the Apostles, grant me the grace, that my soule may not be infected. with the ill habits of pernicious men, and that I be not found among them, when vengeance falleth vpō their heads.

Signe my Forehead with the Seale of your holy grace, that the An-

M   gell

gell, when he ſtriketh,
may abſtaine from hur-
ting me, as he did from
the firſt borne of thoſe
houſes of Egypt which
were marked vpon the
poſtes of the doores with
the letter T, the preſigu-
ratiue ſigne of our Re-
demption.

2. Take me away like
Suſanna from the Adul-
terers, and make me ſoo-
ner to chooſe death, then
to giue conſent to their

diſor

disordinate cocupiscence; for if I be vniustly iudged by men, god will change the iniquity of their sentence.

Separate me like vnto Daniel, from the Idolaters; for my soule shall be more safe among the Lyons clawes, then in assisting at their Sacrifices, and in adoring with them the Creature, & wholy forsaking the Creatour.

Grant

Grant me accesse wth those who do call vpon your holy Name, & who put their trust in you, for with them I shall commit no euill; and I shall participate of your grace, when you make it flow vpon them.

3. I will visit often your holy Churches, to the end, that being in the company of those who serue your maiesty, I may sing with profoūd

humi-

humility the merits of your praises.

All you who haue your hearts aright, and the honour of this Virgin in singular respect and recommendation, draw neare vnto me, & we will blesse her altogether, for she will willingly giue eare vnto our prayers, and will grant vs our petitions.

Blessed be the Father and Mother who haue

M 3 brought

brought you foorth in-
to the world; and Blef-
fed alfo be the breafts,
which haue giuen you
fucke, for they haue layd
the foundation of our
Saluation, fince from
your facred wombe hath
iffued Chrift IESVS the
Sauiour of the world

4. Be he Bleffed who
hath factified you from
your Mothers wombe,
and hath made you to
proceed pure, & cleane

from

from originall sinne, by the priuiledge of Grace; and Blessed be the Lynage, from whence you are descended.

Blessed be the Holy Ghost, who hath ouershaddowed you; since that your fruitfulnes hath beene the cause of our saluation, & by you the Heauens haue bene opened vnto vs, & Paradise hath byn made our inheritance.

Praise

Praise this Holy Virgin, O all yee Angeils of God: O all yee Apostles, Martyrs, Confessours, and Blessed Soules in Heauen praise & magnify her likewise; and we who inhabite heere vnder your feet, will blesse and praise her, all the dayes of our life.

5. Blessed be the Name of Mary, both in Heauen, and Earth, and let all honour be giuen

ther-

thereunto from hence-
forth for euermore : for
this Name is terrible &
fearefull to the euill spirits, but sweet & health-
full to those who call
vpon it .

Blessed be he likewise
who shall put his hope
in her, and cursed be the
detractour of her praise;
since that her merits are
greater then any tongue
of man can expresse , or
voyce sufficiétly declare.

M 5   . Giue

6. Giue me grace to frequent the company of vertuous people , and to shun the vicious ; for those who frequent the euill, shall become euill; & those who dwell with the theefe, shall become theeues; and they who haunt the peruerse, will become like vnto them, and the concupiscence of their owne flesh will carry them away.

Those who touch

pitch,

pitch, shall be defiled, and thofe who bath in the Riuer will be wett; Euen fo thofe who keep depraued company, can get no good amóg them, and thofe who frequent the good, cánot do euill in their company.

At the houre of your departure out of this life, you were affifted by all the moft faithfull friends and feruants of our Lord IESVS Chrift

your

your Sonne : the ayre
made them way, & from
diuers places & regions
of the earth, they all af-
sembled to honour your
funeralls, and to be the
witnesses of your glo-
rious Assumption.

7. Grant me this grace
(O most fauourable Vir-
gin) that I may haue no
acquaintance or familia-
rity with those, who are
cōtemners of your holy
Name, nor euer to keep

them

them company.

I haue said in my heart, I had rather be the Child of the poore man who feareth god, & serueth his holy Mother; then to be the Brother, & sole Heire of the rich, who putteth all his trust in his riches, and negle-cteth the seruice of christ Iesvs, and of the Blessed Virgin Mary.

Keepe me alwaies in this mynd, and let me

rather

rather choose to conuerse with the simple in humility, thé with the wicked in pride and statelines; for so much as the vanityes of this world passe away, but the humble are rewarded with an immortall recópence in heauen.

8. Assist me with your Grace, endow me with the vertue of your Chastity, strengthen me with your Patience, arme me

with

with your Constancy, behold me with your pittifull Eye, compasse me about with your Mercy, and giue me a glympse of your glory: for these vertues are all the Companions, with which I desire to be associated.

I will speake with you alone, & will pray vnto you in all Humility. Oh how excellent will this company be? Giue eare

fauou-

fauourably vnto me, &
withdraw not your felfe
away from me, becaufe
of the foulenes of my of-
fences.

9. Comfort my heart
by the fweetnes of your
charitable Piety, for I
am your Seruant; and
from my infancy haue
I vowed my felfe vnto
your feruice, euer to ac-
knowledg & adore you:
and thofe who hate your
Name, are greiued that

1

I haue anſwered them againe, That they are nothing in regard of thoſe which are due vnto you, & that all the Angels togeather haue not eloquence inough to vtter the leaſt part of thé.

10. I haue heard my Predeceſſours ſay, who ſayd likewiſe, that they had heard it from their fore-Fathers, that your Miracles were great and admirable, ouer all the

worl d,

world, .and that thofe whom you affift, & help, were alwaies happy and Bleffed in the end.

I haue giuen credit to their wordes, and haue taught the fame to my pofterity; grāt me grace to haue a particular feeling of your ayd, & that at the end my dayes, I may be receiued into Heauen, in the company of the Bleffed foules in Paradife.

THE

THE HYMNE
Extremum claudens.

THe Virgins admirable yeares,
   Now drawing fast vnto their
   end,
And death appearing with no feares
   Which might her sweet repose
   offend:
A gentle wynd along the ayre,
   Sent out by Gods especiall grace,
Made all th' Apostles to repaire
   From sundry parts vnto that place.
Among this noble Company,
   The Angels from th' heauens des-
   cending,

                    Sunge

Sunge forth full sweet and ioyfully
  This following hymne before her
    ending.
O Come away (Queene most desired)
  Vnto your place in heauen so high,
Which longetime since hath bene pre-
    pared,
  For your Immortality.
Aboue the Azure Vault of Hea'uen,
  Her sweet soule then departed
    straight,
By which assured signe was giuen,
  Of wondrous ioy did her awayt.
All Glory euer be to you
  Sweet IESVS, Blessed Maries
    Sonne,
The like vnto the Father too,
  And holy Ghost, whilst ages
    runne.

THE

THE FOVRTENTH
PETITION.

Aue Maria gratia plena Dominus
tecū, benedicta tu in mulieribus,
& benedictus fructus ventris tuī
I E S V S. Sancta Maria mater Dei,
ora pro nobis &c.

Mary, Mary, Mary,	
Mary, Mary, Mary,	
Mary, Mary, Mary,	
Mary, Mary, Mary,	Blessed Vir-
Mary, Mary, Mary,	gin Mary,
Mary, Mary, Mary,	obtaine
Mary, Mary, Mary,	me heere
Mary, Mary, Mary,	n y Purga-
Mary, Mary, Mary,	tory.
Mary, Mary, Mary,	

O

O BLESSED Virgin Mary, who haue a singular care of the saluation of those that call vpon you, procure me my Purgatory heere in this life, and let me feele some part of those afflictiōs which you haue borne, and of the dolours which you haue suffered, during the passion of your deare Sonne Christ IESVS our Blessed Lord and Redeemer.

Permit

Permit me not to be of the number of those who haue all their plea-sure & ease in this world, since it is impossible for them to enioy a double beatitude; for so should God be an vniust distri-buter of his Graces.

2. Those who posses-se the goods of the earth and set their whole affe-ction vpon them, shall be depriued of the king-dome of Heauen; but
the

the poore, & thofe who haue fuffred hunger in this life, shall there be eternally refreshed.

Our eyes cannot behold both Heauen and Earth at once, and whofoeuer cafteth downe his fight too much vpō the earth to pleafe his fenfuality, shall find himfelfe dazelled when he would looke vp on high; & againft his will shall fall into the pitt, where

he)

he hath buryed his treasure.

I will begge of you to send me my punishmét, assoone as I shall haue offended, whether it be of Body, or of Soule, or in my goods, & that I may know when I haue offended, and withall seeke meanes to enter againe into your Grace.

3. I had rather endure all the afflictions of this world then to suffer one

N   houre

houre in Purgatory, since that the paynes of this life, are but pleasures compared with those that be in Hell.

The Afflictions of the liuing can last but for a time; but there is no end in the paines of the damned: and the horrible cruelty therof cannot possibly be expressed.

Preuent by your grace the sinnes which I

may

may commit, and turne
away my will from thé,
that I may not be lyable
to the paynes which are
to follow, and that I be
free from blame and re-
prehenſion.

4. The Heauens are
pure and cleane, and the
Court of Chriſt Iesvs
is onely compoſed of
holy Soules: the wicked
cannot enter in there
vnles they be firſt wa-
ſhed from their ſinns, &

N 2 pur-

purged according to their deserts.

I will afflict my body by fasting, and I will cloath it in haircloath; I will mingle my drinke with teares, & put ashes in my bread, that I may take punishment on my selfe, for the sinnes I haue committed.

Fortify me with a constant Patience (O most Charitable Virgin) to the end I may sustaine

these

these austerityes, for that
they be the fitt medici-
nes, & salues for a soule
grieuously wounded;
and which do keepe it
from the perill of eter-
nall death and damna-
tion.

5. Stir me vp to do
true and profitable Pen-
nance for the remission
of my sinnes; & graunt
that in imitation of the
Niniuites I may con-
uert my selfe vnto you

N 3   with

with teares, falting, and humility of heart.

Grant that I may imitate the holy Prophet Dauid in auftere pennance, for hauing offended God; that fo my foule may appeare faire and cleane before the Throne of his Maiefty; and let him not iudge me according to his Iuftice, but according to his Mercy.

Put before me the

exam-

example of Blessed Mary Magdalen, & inflame my heart to imitate her, for she obteined by long pennáce & good works, a meruailous grace of God; and the pennance wherwith she punished her body, preserued her soule from the fire of Purgatory.

6. Let the teares be neuer dryed vp in myne eyes, and let me eat the bread of dolour, that

my too great felicity
may not make me ingra-
tefull for the Grace of
God , and that being
mixed with afflictions,
may make me fly to
him.

Stir vp in me good
and holy desires, & giue
me grace to put them in
executiõ, becaufe I haue
cryed vnto you in all
humility , and haue of-
fred my vowes vnto you
with fighes & groanes .

7. I

7. I beseech you (O most Sacred Virgin) be pleased to make me passe the course of this life, by the straite and thorny pathes, which lead vnto the celestiall Beatitude; & that I may leaue the beaten way of pleasure & delight vpon my left hand, leaft walking therin I be vnawares caft down headlong into Hell.

You did the same

when

when you were conuer-
sant heere in this world,
since that you tasted of
most bitter dolours; in
reward wherof your B.
Sonne Christ Iesus hath
crowned you Queene of
Heauen, and endowed
you with Eternall Feli-
city in his glory of Pa-
radise.

Giue eare vnto me as
often as I shall call vpō
you, that humane affli-
ctions may not bring

me

me to despaire, and that
I may endure patiently
the iust punishment w^{ch}
I haue merited by my
offences .

8. Cast the beames
of your mercy vpon me,
that they may penetrate
into my heart , and that
the sweetnes of your
Peace, may refresh me
in my torments; to the
end I may worke the sal-
uation of my soule , du-
ring the miserable pil-

gri-

grimage of this life.

I will endure patiently all bodily afflictions, so that you be not offended with me, and that they may turne to the saluation of my soule: for the felicity which it shall enioy, shalbe immortall, since it shall neuer dye; but the afflictions of the body shall haue an end, when we come to depart this life

Suffer not my mouth

(O

(O most louing Virgin)
to be defiled with filthy
and dishonest words;
neyther let my Soule
remaine in euill cogita-
tions, but rather let it
take delight, to meditate
vpon the paines of Pur-
gatory.

9. Strike (O most
sweet Virgin) strike my
heart with the Dart of
true pennance, and let it
be scorched with the fire
of your Charity, that it

may

may wholy dye in you,
and for your loue in-
dure all labour, and tra-
uaile both day & night.

I will keepe my foule
imprifoned in my body,
and will not fuffer it to
take any other delecta-
tion, then in the medi-
tation of your praifes, &
in fending forth conti-
nuall praiers to your fa-
cred Maiefty.

Withdraw not your
fauourable countenance

from

from me, I beseech you, & turne not away your face from me; for feare that being destitute of your Grace, I fall into the Abysme of eternall damnation.

10. Do not suffer (O most sacred Virgin) the heynousnes of my sinnes to cast me into the gulfe of despaire of your mercy; and giue me a firme desire heere to doe pennance for them, that

I

I may not be long detayned in Purgatory

Teach me in this life the way which I ought to goe, that I may ariue at the Port of Saluation, and enioy the eternall Beatitude, and reckon me in the number of the Blessed in Paradise, in the company of Christ IESVS your beloued Sonne, and of your selfe, and of all the Saints there present.

THE

THE HYMNE
Reginæ Cæli è domo.

THE body of the sacred Mayd,
    The which had tasted death
of life,
Within an humble Tombe was layd,
    Low in the Vale of Iosaphat.
But could by no meanes there be
    found,
    When sought for, after three daies
    space,
Where it before was layd in ground,
    But onely Manna left in place.
We do beleeve that Christ in Glory,
    With Angels Quires descended
    there,

An

And that in signe of her victory,
  Both soule and corps to Heauen
    did beare.
Where, by the holy Trinity,
  She was receau'd, and in was led,
And there with Crownes, most glo-
    riously
  They circled in her sacred head.
Mother in honour lifted high,
  And farre aboue all humaine
    race;
O grant vnto me, when I dy,
  There to behold your Glorious face.
All Glory euer be to you
  Sweet IESVS, Blessed Maryes
    Sonne,
The like vnto the Father too,
  And holy Ghost whilst ages runne.

THE

THE FIFTEENTH
PETITION.

Aue Maria gratia plena Dominus tecū, benedicta tu in mulieribus, & benedictus fructus ventris tui Iɛsvs. Sancta Maria mater Dei, ora pro nobis &c.

Mary, Mary, Mary,	
Mary, Mary, Mary,	
Mary, Mary, Mary,	Moſt Bleſ-
Mary, Mary, Mary,	ſed Mary, vouchſafe
Mary, Mary, Mary,	to be my
Mary, Mary, Mary,	Aduocate
Mary, Mary, Mary,	in the day of Iudg-
Mary, Mary, Mary,	ment.
Mary, Mary, Mary,	
Mary, Mary, Mary,	

I

I HAVE yet one more most humble petitiō to present vnto you, O holy Virgin Mary, to desire you that you will grant me the grace, that I may continually call to remembrance the houre of my death, and therby to consider what I am, and what I shall then be, to the end my heart may not be puffed vp with the pride of vaine presumption of

Immor-

Immortality.

May it please you, (O most louing Virgin) to put before mine eyes, the vnclothing of this my Mortall body; and how the same taken out of my exteriour Garments, is no other then a sacke of bones, transparant in an hundred places, and as a dead Carryon abandoned & giuen ouer to wormes, & vermin to feed vpon.

2. Who

2. Who will haue pitty on me when I shall not be able to demand succour of any one? And who will put me out of the way of Passengers, when I shall see them no more? And againe, who will blush at my shame, whé another shall haue discouered me?

Who will do good vnto me, well knowing that I can neuer repay him with the like? And

who

who will draw neare vn-
to me, whē I shall seeme
fearefull, euen to the li
uing? And who will des-
cend downe vnto the
dead, for to lay me there
among them?

3. O most mercifull
Virgin, be pleased then
to haue pitty vpon me,
and raise vp some chari-
table people to couer
my nakednes, and cast
the earth vpō me, when
my freinds & kinsfolkes

forsake

forsake me.

He whom you assist with your Grace, shall not be forsaken, and in the middest of the deserts, he shall find a graue, or els the Lyons shall digge it for him, & laying his body therein, shall after couer it, shewing themselues humanely officious vnto him.

And the fishes of the sea will soouer cast him

out

out like vnto Ionas, then
that his body shall pe-
rish in the waters, if you
do respect him; for your
miracles are great both
in Heauen and Earth, &
your power cannot be
comprehended.

4. Goe therefore (O
my Soule) & enter pro-
foūdly into this thoght;
& since thou art to make
this iourney, thinke be-
fore of the hazards w^ch
thou shalt meet vpon

the

the way, and the peril-
lous dangers into which
thou maieſt fall, after ſo
ſad a departure out of
the priſon of thy body.

And wilt thou not be
afraid, when the knot
which tyes thy ſoule &
body togeather, ſhall be
diſſolued, leaſt that the
horrible aſſaults of thy
Enemyes, may ouer-
come thee? & that their
terrible and fierce ſight
will ſo affright thee, as
to

to make thee giue vp
thy selfe with despaire
into their hands?

5. Wilt thou not feare
to be tossed with the
wynds, and be made to
wander from the right
path by a thousand out-
ragious tempests? and
to fall into the snares of
the euill spirits, who will
cast thee headlong into
the depth of Hell?

Whither wilt thou go
poore Soule? Or what

place

place is there so secret
which can hide thee,
from this great Iudge of
man? In what wilt thou
put thy trust? and what
wilt thou carry out of
this world with thee,
that may serue to ran-
some thee from thine
enemyes?

6. Ponder now ther-
fore,and diligently con-
sider euery one of thy
workes by it selfe, and
cast vp the accompt of
                      thy

thy life , to see if thy good Workes may recompence thy euill: for thou must satisfy for all, or els thou shalt be deliuered to thine enemies who ar the executioners of the Iustice of God.

Take the holy Virgin Mary, for thy Aduocate in this life , that she may know thee, and plead thy cause at that houre, before her Sonne Christ IESVS: giue vnto

O 3　　　　her

her the Honour which she deserueth, and seeke by al meanes her friendship, whilest thou art heere.

Whosoeuer shall be supported by her heauenly Power, shall be sure neuer to fall; & he who hath part in her Grace, shall find consolation in all his necessityes, and God will iudge him according to his Mercy, and make him

par-

partaker of the glory of
Paradife.

7. Take me vnder
the shaddow of your
wyngs; arme your right
hand to defend me, that
mine enemies may not
erect their Trophyes of
me, and reioyce at my
fad fortune.

Clofe you vp mine
eyes, at the hower of
death, that I may not fee
the fearefull and vgly
shapes of the euill fpi-

O 4 rits,

rits , but dazell them
with the beames of your
grace, and with the sight
of Angels which it may
please you to send , to be
then present , and to af
sist me

Let the brightnes of
your glory put to flight
the Prince of darkenes;
I haue made no Coue-
nant with him : he seeks
somewhat of me , and I
owe nothing vnto him;
for in you alone I haue

put

put my truſt, and vnto you alone I haue engaged & aſſured my Soule.

8 I put it into your hands, deale with it according to your Mercy, and demaund of your ſweet Sonne that which may be moſt needfull for it, becauſe it will be ſo aſtoniſhed at the greatnes of his maieſty, and ſo confuſed at the greiuouſnes of its owne ſinnes, that it will not

O 5   dare

dare to appeare before him.

Grant (O moſt holy Virgin) that the cogitation of death may come often into my mind, to the end, it may diuert me frō ſinne, for therin is no euill; and it is not the dart of death which makes vs dye eternally, but our owne ſinns and iniquities.

Death onely ſeparates the ſoule and the body,

and

and is of it selfe nothing,
for your deare Sonne
Christ IESVS himselfe
hath beene pleased to
take vpon him humane
flesh in you, therby to
tast of death; and hath
likewise permitted you
to passe the same way.

9. I beseech you par-
ticulerly to exempt me
from Eternall death: &
as for the temporall, I
attend it at your good
pleasure, and would wil-

lingly

lingly come to you into the Glory of Paradise with the reſt of the Bleſſed Soules, there to enioy the preſence of my Bleſſed Sauiour, and your Selfe.

My ſtay heere doth much afflict me, when I conſider the miſeryes of this world, and thinke vpon the contentment that they haue who are neere vnto you: my Predeceſſours, and all thoſe

who

who were most deare
vnto me in this world,
do already sing forth
your praises with the
Blessed Soules , vnto
which happynes I like-
wise do aspire.

10. Grant me then
this particuler Grace, to
keepe my selfe alwayes
vpright, and that I be
not like to those, who
fall vpon their owne
sword, and kill themsel-
ues; for there is no death

but

but vnto thofe who dye in their finnes, without Confeffion and Pennance.

Be pleafed with my prayers (O moft facred Virgin Mary :) and may it pleafe you not to reiect this little Pfalter dedicated to your Sacred Maiefty, a part wherof I will euery day recite before you, to the end you may receaue my Soule into your bofome, when

it

it shall depart out of this world, to paſſe vnto the other life.

THE HYMNE
Salue Regina.

To you, O ſoueraigne Queene, all hayle,
    All hayle of Mercy Mother deare,
Our life, our hope, our ſweetnes hayle,
    To you we ſinners do draw neare.
To you, we ſonnes of Eue do cry,
    To you we ſigh, we weepe, we groane,
Who in the vale of teares do lye,
    Making to you our piteous moane.

O

O therfore you our Aduocate,
    Those your sweet Eyes of pitty
        turne.
Vpon our miserable state,
    Of euery one (but you) forlorne.
And after this our exile past,
    Grant, we beseech, that we may
        come
Sweet IESVS *for to see at last,*
    The Blessed fruite of your blest
        wombe.
O Virgin full of Clemency,
    O pious Virgin Mary sweet;
Pray for vs al, that worthily
    We Christs true promises may
        meet.

THE

THE
LETANIES OF
OVR B. LADY
OF LORETO.

LORD haue mercy
on vs. Chriſt
haue mercy on vs.
Lord haue mercy on vs.
O Chriſt heare vs.
O Chriſt gracioufly he-
are vs.
God the Father of hea-

uen,

ué, haue mercy on vs.
God the Sonne, Redee-
mer of the World,
haue mercy on vs.
God the Holy Ghoſt,
haue mercy on vs.
Holy Trinity one God,
haue mercy on vs.

Holy Mary,
Holy Mother of
God,
Holy Virgin of
Virgins,
Mother of Chriſt,
Mother of diuine

Pray for vs.

grace,

grace,
Most pure Mother,
Most chast mother,
Vndefiled Mother,
Vntouched Mother
Louely Mother,
Admirable Mother
Mother of the Cre-
    atour,
Mother of our Sa-
    uiour,
Most prudét virgin
Venerable Virgin,
Virgin worthy of
    prayse,

Pray for vs.

Potent

Potent Virgin,
Clement Virgin,
Faithfull Virgin,
Mirrour of Iuſtice,
Seate of wiſedome,
Cauſe of our Ioy,
Spirituall Veſſell,
Honourable Veſſel,
Noble Veſſel of de-
uotion,
Myſticall Roſe,
Tower of Dauid,
Tower of Iuory,
Golden Houſe,
Arke of Couenant,

Pray for vs.

Gate

Gate of heauen,
Morning starre,
Health of the sick,
Refuge of sinners,
Comfortresse of
   the afflicted,
The help of Chri-
   stians,
Queen of Angells,
Queen of Patriarks
Queen of Prophets
Queen of the Apo-
   stles,
Queen of Martyrs,
Queen of Confes-
          sours,

Pray for vs.

ſours,

Queene of Vir-
gins,

Queen of al Saints.

}　Pray for.

Lambe of God, who takeſt away the ſinnes of the world, Spare vs, O Lord.

Lambe of God &c Heare vs, O Lord.

Lambe of God &c. Haue mercy on vs.

O Chriſt heare vs.

O Chriſt gratiouſly hea-
re vs.

Lord

Lord haue mercy on vs.
chriſt haue mercy on vs.
Lord haue mercy on vs.
Our Father &c.

Verſ. And lead vs not
into temptation.

Reſp. But deliuer vs
from euill.

Verſ. O Lord heare my
prayer.

Reſp. And let my cry
come vnto thee.

Let vs pray.

VVE beſeech thee,
O Lord, powre

forth

forth thy grace into our harts : that we who haue known the incarnatiõ of Chriſt thy Sonne, the Angel declaring it, may be brought by his Paſſion and Croſſe , vnto the Glory of Reſurrection . Throgh the ſame Chriſt our Lord. Amen .

FINIS.

THE
LITTLE OFFICE
OF THE
ALL·IMMACVLATE
CONCEPTION
OF OVR B. LADY.

To be dayly fayd by fuch as are deuoted to this diuine Myftery.

AT MATTINS.

Verf. Oh, let my lipps fing, and difplay.

Refp. The Bleſſed Vir-

P   gins

gins praiſe this day.

Verſ. O Lady to my helpe intend.

Reſp. Me from my foes ſtrongly defend.

Verſ. Glory be to the Father, & to the Son, & to the holy Ghoſt.

Reſp. Euen as it was in the beginning, & now & euer, and world without end. Amen.

The *Hymne.*

H Ayle Lady of the world,

Of

Of heaué bright Queen,
Hayle Virgin of virgins,
Starre early seene.
    Hayle full of all grace,
Cleere light diuine:
Lady, to succour vs,
With speed incline.
    God from Eternity
Before all other,
Of the Word thee ordai-
To be the Mother, (ned
    Wherwith he created
The earth, sea, and skye:
His fayre spouse he chose
    thee,

From Adams finne free.

Verf. God hath elected, and preelected her.

Refp. He hath made her dwell in his tabernacle.

Let vs pray.

O Holy Mary, Mother of our Lord Iefus Chrift, Queene of Heauen, & Lady of the world, who forfakeft or defpifeft none ; behold me mercifully with the eye of Pitty, and obtaine for me of thy beloued

Sonne

Sonne, pardon of all my
finnes : that I who with
deuout affection do now
honour thy holy Cōcep-
tion, may heereafter en-
ioy the reward of Eter-
nall bliſſe; through the
grace and mercy of our
Lord Ieſus Chriſt, whom
thou (a Virgin) dideſt
bring forth . Who with
the Father, & the Holy
Ghoſt, liueth and raig-
neth, one God, in per-
fect Trinity, for euer

and euer . Amen.

Verſ. O Lady heare my prayer.

Reſp. And let my crye come vnto thee.

Verſ. Let vs bleſſe our Lord.

Reſp. Thanks be to God.

Verſ. And let the ſoules of the faithful departed, through the mercy of God, reſt in peace.

Reſp. Amen.

Aт Pʀɪᴍᴇ. (tend.

O Lady to my help in-

Me

Resp. Me from my foes
    strongly defend.
Verf. Glory be to the &c
    The Hymne.

Hayle Virgin moſt
    prudent,
Houſe for God plac't:
With the ſeauenfold pil-
And Table grac't. (lar,
  Sau'd from contagion
Of the frayle earth:
In wombe of thy parent,
Saint before byrth.
  Mother of the liuing,
Gate of Saints merits:

The new Star of Iacob,
Queene of pure spirits.
  To Zabulon fearefull,
Armes array:
Be thou of Christians
Refuge and stay.
Verf. He hath created
  her in his holy spirit.
Resp. And hath powred
  her out , ouer all his
  workes.

    Let vs pray.

O Holy Mary, Mother of our Lord,
&c.

                    Verf.

Verf. O Lady heare my
    prayer.

Resp. And let my crye
    come vnto thee. &c.

AT THIRD.

O Lady, to my helpe
    intend.

Resp. Me from my foes
    ftrongly defend.

Verf. Glory be to the &c.

The Hymne.

H Ayle Arke of Coue-
    nant,

Throne, Salomõs fame,

Bright rainbow of heauẽ

Bush fate inflame.

The fleece of Gedeon,
The flowring Rod,
Sweet hony of Sampfon
Clofet of God.

T'was meet Sonne fo
noble
Should faue frō ftayne,
(Wherwith al Eues chil-
Spotted remaine) (dren
The maid whome for
He had elected, (Mother
Thatshe might be neuer
With finne infected.

Ver. I dwel in the higheft.

Refp.

Resp. And my throne is in the pillar of the cloud.

Let vs pray.

O Holy Mary Mother of our &c.

Vers. O Lady heare my prayer.

Res. And let my crye &c.

AT SIXT.

O Lady, to my helpe intend.

Resp. Me from my foes strongly defend.

Vers. Glory be to the &c.

The

The *Hymne*.

HAyle Mother & Vir-
gin,
  Of the Trinity
Temple, Ioy of Angels,
Cell of Purity.
  Comfort of Mourners
Guarden of pleasure:
Palme-tree of Patience,
Chastityes treasure.
  Thou Land Sacerdo-
Art blessed, holy,   (tall
From sinne Originall
Exempted solely.
  Citty of the Highest,

Gate

Gate of the East:
Virgins gemme, in thee
All Graces rest.

verſ. As the Lilly amõg
thornes:

Reſp. So my beloued a-
mong the daughters
of Adam.

Let *vs pray.*

O Holy Mary mother
of our Lord &c.

verſ. O Lady heare my
prayer.

Reſp. And let my crye
&c.

A T

AT NINTH.

O Lady to my helpe in-
tend.

Resp. Me from my foes
strongly defend.

vers. Glory be to &c.

The Hymne.

H Aile Citty of refuge,
King Dauids tower,
Fensed with bulwarkes,
And armours power.

In thy Conception
Charity did flame:
The fierce Dragós pride
Was brought to shame.

Iudith

Iudith inuincible,
Woman of Armes:
Fayre Abisai Virgin,
True Dauid warmes.

Sonne of faire Rachel
Did Ægypt store:
Mary, of the World
The Sauiour bore.

Verf. Thou art all fayre,
O my beloued.

Reʃp. And originall ʃpot
was neuer in thee.

Let *vs pray.*

O Holy Mary, mother
of our Lord &c.

verʃ,

verſ O Lady heare my prayer.

Reſp. And let my cry &c.

AT EVENSONGE.

O Lady to my helpe intend.

Reſp. Me from my foes ſtrongly defend.

verſ. Glory to be the Father &c.

The Hymne.

HAyle Dyall, in which Turnes retrograde

The Sunne ten degrees,

The Word is fleſh made

That

That man frō Hell-pit
T'heauen might rise,
Th' Immense lesse then
   Angels,
In stable lyes.
  This Sun did on Mary
Betimes appeare:
Made her Conception,
A morning cleere.
    Faire Lilly mongst
   thornes.
That Serpent frights:
Cleere Moone that in
  darke
The wanderer lights.

verſ. In heauen, I made a neuer-fayling light arife.

Reſp. And I couered all the world as a myſt

Let *vs pray.*

O Holy Mary, mother of our Lord &c.

verſ. O Lady heare my prayer.

Reſp. And let my crye &c.

AT COMPLINE.

LEt thy Sonne Chriſt Ieſus, O Lady, paci-

fyed

fyed by thy prayers, conuert vs.

Resp. And turne his anger away from vs.

verf. O Lady to my help intend.

Resp. Me from my foes ſtrongly defend.

verf. Glory be to the Father &c.

The Hymne.

HAyle floriſhing Virgin,
Chaſtities renowne:
Queene of Clemency,

Whom

Whom stars do crowne.
  Thou pure aboue An-
    gels,
Doest Sonne behould :
Sits at his right hand,
Attyred in gould.
  Mother of grace, Hope
To men afraid :
Bright starre of the sea,
In shipwracke ayde.
    Graunt Heauen-gate
      open,
That by thee blest:
We thy Sonne may see,
In blissefull rest.

vers.

verf. Thy Name, O Mary, is like sweet Oyle powred out.

Resp. Thy feruants haue loued thee exceedingly.

Let vs pray.

O Holy Mary, mother our Lord &c.

verf. O Lady heare my prayer.

Resp. And let my crye come vnto thee.

Verf. Let vs bleffe our Lord.

Resp. Thanks be to God.

verf.

ver. And let the foules of
the faithfull &c.

Resp. Amen.

THE COMMENDATION.

TO thee pious Virgin,
We humbly prefent
These houres Canonicall
With pure intent.
Guide pilgrimes, vntill
VVith Chrift we meet :
In our agony ayde vs.
O Mary fweet. Amen.

Pope Paul the V. hath graunted an hū-
dred dayes of Indulgence , to thofe who
shal fay this Ant-hymne, & Prayer fol-
lowing.

Antiph.

Antiph· This is the brāch, in which was neither knot of originall , nor barke of actuall ſin foūd·

Verſ. In thy Conception, O Virgin , thou waſt immaculate·

Reſp . Pray vnto the Father for vs, whoſe Son thou didſt bring forth.

Let vs pray·

O God, who by the immaculate Conceptiō of the Virgin, didſt prepare a fit habitation for

thy

thy Sonne; VVe befeech
thee, that as by the fore-
fight of the death of the
fame her Son , thou didft
preferue her pure from
all fpot:fo likewife graūt,
that we, by her intercef-
fion made free from fin,
may attaine vnto thee.
Through our Lord Iefus
Chrift thy Sonne &c.
who liueth & raigneth
one God, world without
end . Amen ·

FINIS.